FRANZ KAFKA

MODERN MASTERS

MODERN MASTERS

EDITED BY frank kermode

franz
kafka

erich heller

NEW YORK | THE VIKING PRESS

833.912

Kllhe

Published in 1975 in a hardbound and paperbound edition by
The Viking Press, Inc., 625 Madison Avenue,
New York, N.Y. 10022

LIBRARY OF CONGRESS CATALOGING IN PUBLICATION DATA
Heller, Erich, 1911-
Franz Kafka.
(Modern masters)
Bibliography: p.
Includes index.
1. Kafka, Franz, 1883-1924—Criticism and interpretation
PT2621.A26Z74624   833'.9'12   74-34020
ISBN 0-670-32721-2
ISBN 0-670-01987-9 pbk.

Printed in U.S.A.

Acknowledgment is made to the following for
permission to quote material:
ALFRED A. KNOPF, INC.: From *The Trial* by Franz Kafka,
translated by Willa and Edwin Muir,
Copyright 1937, © 1956 and renewed 1965 by
Alfred A. Knopf, Inc. From *The Castle* by Franz Kafka,
translated by Willa and Edwin Muir.
Copyright 1930, 1954 and renewed 1958 by
Alfred A. Knopf, Inc. Reprinted by
permission of the publisher.
SCHOCKEN BOOKS INC.: From *Briefe* by Franz Kafka.
Copyright © 1958 by Schocken Books, Inc., from
Letter to His Father by Franz Kafka.
Copyright © 1953, 1954 by Schocken Books Inc.,
from *Letters to Felice* by Franz Kafka.
Copyright © 1967, 1973 by Schocken Books Inc.,
from *Diaries 1910-1923* by Franz Kafka.
Copyright © 1948 by Schocken Books, Inc.,
from *Diaries 1914-1923* by Franz Kafka.
Copyright © 1949 by Schocken Books Inc.,
from *The Penal Colony* by Franz Kafka.
Copyright © 1948 by Schocken Books Inc.,
from *The Great Wall of China* by Franz Kafka.
Copyright © 1946 by Schocken Books Inc.,
from *Dearest Father* by Franz Kafka.
Copyright © 1954 by Schocken Books Inc.
All reprinted by permission of Schocken Books Inc.

FOR B. J. W.

P R E F A C E

A glance at any bibliography of writings on Kafka shows
how problematic it is to add to the superabundance of
books and articles on him. It would of course be arro-
gance simply to say that the present writer offers a
radically new interpretation of the works of an author
who partly has himself to blame for the massive interpretative superstructure that has been built on the
comparatively slender base of his stories and unfinished
novels; only partly, because much of it can be ascribed
to the laws of a highly industrialized academe, a producer society the wheels of which are relentlessly kept
in motion more often than not without any regard to
true intellectual demands. Kafka's share of the blame
lies in his being the creator of the most obscure lucidity
in the history of literature, a phenomenon that, like a
word one has on the tip of one's tongue, perpetually
attracts and at the same time repels the search for what
it is and means.

If in this inflationary situation only an arrogant interpreter would claim to have any staggeringly new insights, it would yet be false modesty to introduce a book on Kafka by saying that one might just as well not have written it. My contribution, for what it is worth, originates in a long familiarity with his works and, if this does not sound too presumptuous, with the mind behind the work, an acquaintance made perhaps a little more intimate by the facts of cultural geography. It is my hope that this, if nothing else, gives some legitimacy to this book.

I wrote on Kafka long before any thought of the present volume, and as what I wrote in the past not only seemed to me still valid but impressed me as being of one piece with my later reflections, I have not hesitated to let it play its natural part within the new book's purview and unity. This applies above all to my essay on Kafka in *The Disinherited Mind* and to the introduction that I wrote more recently to an edition of his letters to Felice Bauer, an extraordinarily comprehensive self-documentation of a mind torn between the desire "to live" and that of "dying to life" in the consuming service of his vocation: the art of literature. As this dilemma, suffered in every conceivable and sometimes inconceivable variation, is always near the center of Kafka's work and existence, its exposition and meditation was bound to become one of the unifying themes of this book. It may well be that it is this conflict, apparently idiosyncratic but in its wider implications touching upon a universal irresolution of the modern sensibility, that gives to Kafka's works the qualities of both the unique *and* the representative. Together they make for a classic; and what Kafka in his uniqueness represents, is indeed the mind of an age. It would be a distressing task to have to draw with any exactitude, as if one were its land surveyor, the geographical and historical boundaries of that age. Its first major literary document was perhaps Dostoevski's *Notes from the Underground*, and to read Kafka is to realize that we still belong to his epoch if we have not altogether ceased to belong anywhere.

Throughout these pages I have refrained from quoting what has been written about Kafka; or from quarreling with my predecessors; or from applauding them. This indeed does not mean that I regard them all as negligible. On the contrary, I have learned much from the minority I have read—either from the consent they inspired or often by the opposition they evoked. But to name them not only would be invidious in its unavoidable selectivity but would also clutter up these pages and even deprive them of whatever immediate responsiveness they possess: the responsiveness of this one reader to Kafka. Those to whom I am indebted, often no doubt without realizing it, will easily recognize their share and may be sure of my gratitude.

My thanks for permission to reprint previously published material are due to Messrs. Bowes and Bowes Ltd., London, and Schocken Books Ltd., New York. In addition, Schocken Books have kindly allowed me to quote from their English translations of Kafka's works.

References to Nietzsche's works are, in my own translations, to *Gesammelte Werke* (Munich: Musarion-Ausgabe, 1920–1929). The numbers of volume and page are given in parentheses following the quotations.

Kafka's works, not the incidents of his life, are the focus of this study: or, rather, Kafka's life only insofar as it *is* his writing. Hence there is no biographical introduction. Instead, a fairly detailed Biographical Note is included.

So far as Kafka's works are concerned, I have quoted

from the editions listed in the fourth section of the Short Bibliography, and in the case of the stories entirely from *The Complete Stories*. Most of the quoted aphorisms come from the volume *Dearest Father*, mainly from the section "Reflections on Sin, Suffering, Hope, and the True Way." Passages from Kafka's diaries and letters are specified by their dates, and the passages from the novels can, I believe, easily be located: those from *The Trial* by the connections that exist between the named characters or described situations and the chapter headings; those from *The Castle* by the Roman numerals in parentheses after the quotations, which refer to the numbered chapters.

Erich Heller

Northwestern University
Evanston, Illinois
September 1974

CONTENTS

BIOGRAPHICAL NOTE

1883	Franz Kafka born in Prague July 3, son of Hermann (1852–1931) and Julie (*née* Löwy) (1856–1934).
1889–93	Elementary school at Fleischmarkt.
1889, 1890, 1892	Birth of sisters Elli, Valli, Ottla. Two younger brothers died in infancy.
1893–1901	German gymnasium, Prague; friendship with Oskar Pollak. Family resides in Zeltnergasse.
ca. 1899–1900	Reads Spinoza, Darwin, Nietzsche. Friendship with Hugo Bergman.
1899–1903	Early writings (destroyed).
1901–06	Studies German literature, then law, at German University, Prague.
1902	Vacations in Schelesen and Triesch with Dr. Siegfried Löwy. Meets Max Brod; friendship with Felix Weltsch and Oskar Baum.
1903	Works on a novel, *The Child and the City* (lost).
1903–04	"Description of a Struggle."
1905–06	Summers in Zuckmantel. Love affair with

	an unnamed woman. Meetings with Oskar Baum, Max Brod, Felix Weltsch.
1906	Works in the law office of Richard Löwy, Prague. June: receives degree of doctor juris at German University, Prague. From October: one year's internship in the law courts.
1907–08	Writes "Wedding Preparations in the Country" (fragments of a novel).
1907	October: position in Prague with Assicurazioni Generali, an Italian insurance company. Family moves to Niklas-Strasse.
1908	Takes position at the semigovernmental Workers' Accident Insurance Institute (until retirement, July 1922). Close friendship with Max Brod. Writes "On Mandatory Insurance in the Construction Industry."
1909	Publication of eight prose pieces—parts of the later volume *Betrachtung*—in the Munich literary journal *Hyperion*. September: at Riva and Brescia with Max and Otto Brod. Writes "The Aeroplanes at Brescia."
1910	Member of circle of intellectuals (Mrs. Berta Fanta). March: publication of five prose pieces in Prague German newspaper *Bohemia*. May: beginning of the *Diaries* (quarto notebooks; last entry, June 12, 1923). Yiddish theater company from Eastern Europe performs in Prague. October: Paris, with Max and Otto Brod. December: Berlin.
1911	January–February: business trip to Friedland and Reichenberg. Summer: Zurich, Lugano, Milan, Paris with Max Brod. Plans to write a novel with Brod, *Richard and Samuel*. In a sanatorium in Erlenbach near Zurich. Travel diaries. Writes "Measures to Prevent Accidents [in Factories and Farms]" and "Workers' Accident Insurance and Management."

1911–12	Winter: Yiddish theater company. Friendship with Yiddish actor Isak Löwy; study of Jewish folklore; beginning of a sketch on Löwy.
1911–14	Works on *Amerika* (main parts written 1911–12).
1912	Studies Judaism (H. Graetz, M. I. Pines). February: gives lecture on the Yiddish language. July: Weimar with Max Brod, then alone in the Harz Mountains (Sanatorium Just). Meets Ernst Rowohlt and Kurt Wolff, at that time joint managers of Rowohlt Verlag. August 13: meets Felice Bauer in the house of Max Brod's father in Prague. August 14: manuscript of *Betrachtung* (*Meditation*) sent to publisher. September 20: beginning of correspondence with Felice Bauer. September 22–23: writes "The Judgment." September–October: writes "The Stoker" (or "The Man Who Disappeared"), which later became first chapter of *Amerika*. October 1912–February 1913: gap in the diaries. November: writes "The Metamorphosis."
1913	January: publication of *Betrachtung* (*Meditation*). February 1913–July 1914: lacuna in productivity. Easter: first visit to Felice Bauer in Berlin. Spring: publication of *The Judgment* and "The Stoker." September: journey to Vienna, Venice, Riva. At Riva, friendship with "the Swiss girl." November: Meets Grete Bloch, friend of Felice Bauer, and begins correspondence with her.
1914	Easter: in Berlin. April 12: engagement to Felice Bauer in Berlin. June 1: official engagement reception in Berlin. July 12: engagement broken. Summer: writes "Memoirs of the Kalda Railroad"; goes to Hellerau, Lübeck, Marienlyst on the Baltic with Ernst Weiss. October: writes "In the

Penal Colony." Fall: begins writing *The Trial*. Winter: writes "Before the Law" (part of *The Trial*).

1915   January: renewed meeting with Felice Bauer (in Bodenbach). Continues working on *The Trial*. Receives Fontane Prize for "The Stoker." February: moves from parents' home into rented rooms at Bilekgasse and Langegasse. Journey to Hungary with sister Elli. November: publication of "The Metamorphosis." December (and January 1916): writes "The Village Schoolmaster" ("The Giant Mole").

1916   July: meeting with Felice Bauer in Marienbad. August 20: draws up a list of reasons for and against marriage. Writes stories, later collected in *A Country Doctor*. Winter: moves to Alchemists' Lane in the Castle district of Prague.

1917   Writes "The Hunter Gracchus." Learns Hebrew. Spring: writes "The Great Wall of China." July: second engagement to Felice Bauer. August: begins coughing blood. September 4: Diagnosis of tuberculosis; moves to sister Ottla in Zürau. September 12: leave of absence from office. November 10: Diary entries break off. End of December: breaking off of second engagement to Felice Bauer. Fall–winter: writes aphorisms (Octavo Note-Books).

1918   January–June: Zürau. Reads Kierkegaard. Spring: continues writing aphorisms. Prague, Turnau. November: in Schelesen, meets Julie Wohryzek, daughter of a synagogue custodian. A project for "The Society of Poor Workers," an ascetic society.

1919   January 10: resumes diary, and in spring returns to Prague. (Felice Bauer is married.) Engagement to Julie Wohryzek (broken off in November). May: publication of *In the Penal Colony*. Fall: publication of *A Country Doctor*. November: writes "Letter to His Father." Winter: writes "He," collection of aphorisms; goes to Schelesen with Max Brod.

1920   January 1920–October 15, 1921: gap in diaries. Sick leave from Workers' Accident Insurance Institute. Meets Gustav Janouch and Milena Jesenská-Pollak, Czech writer (Vienna), Meran. Correspondence with Milena. Summer and fall: Prague, writes stories. December: goes to Tatra Mountains (Matliary), meets Robert Klopstock.

1921   October 15: note in diary that all his diaries are being given to Milena. Tatra Mountains sanatorium; then Prague.

1921–24   Writes stories later included in the volume *A Hunger Artist*.

1922   January–September: writes *The Castle*. Spring: writes the story "A Hunger Artist." May: last meeting with Milena. End of June–September: in Planá on the Luschnitz with sister Ottla. Summer: writes "Investigations of a Dog."

1923   July: in Müritz with sister Elli, in a vacation camp of the Berlin Jewish People's Home meets Dora Dymant (Diamant). End of September: with Dora in Berlin–Steglitz; later moves with her to Grunewaldstrasse. Attends lectures at the Berlin Academy for Jewish Studies. Winter: writes "The Burrow." Moves with Dora to Berlin–Zehlendorf. Sends *A Hunger Artist* to publisher.

1924   Spring: writes "Josephine the Singer, or the Mouse Folk." Brought as a patient from Berlin to Prague. April 10: to Wiener Wald Sanatorium; then sanatorium in Kierling, near Vienna, accompanied by Dora and Robert Klopstock.

	June 3: death in Kierling; burial June 11 in the Jewish cemetery in Prague–Straschnitz. Publication of *A Hunger Artist*.
1942	Death of K.'s sister Ottla in Auschwitz. The other two sisters also perished in German concentration camps.
1944	Death of Grete Bloch at the hands of National Socialists. Death of Milena in a German concentration camp.
1952	August: death of Dora Dymant in London.
1960	Death of Felice Bauer.

Punishments and Playthings *de Profundis*

i

1

A reliable witness reports that after the appearance of "The Metamorphosis" in November 1915 —after the announcement, as it were, that a commercial traveler called Gregor Samsa found himself transformed, upon awakening one morning, into a huge insect—Kafka asked an old acquaintance, his Hebrew teacher, whom he happened to meet in the street: "What do you think of the terrible things that go on in our family?" And when he read "The Judgment" to a circle of friends (diary of February 12, 1913), one of his sisters exclaimed, "It is our house," to which he replied—instantly, it seems—"In that case, then, Father would have to be living in the toilet." Despite the sister's mistake about their domestic arrangements, he too felt obviously very much "at home" in the setting of "The Judgment."

The vicinity of literature and autobiography could hardly be closer than it is with Kafka; indeed, it almost amounts to identity. Although in this form it is peculiar to him, it seems at the same time the climax of a chapter in literary history: the history of German writing done in Prague by the predominantly Jewish writers of Kafka's generation. What he said of himself in a letter to Felice, "I *am* literature," is a Prague identification, even if none of the writers of that city was as good as Kafka. Certainly, the sense of being an outsider, of having no existence except a literary one, was no prerogative of the "Prague School": the complaint was known in Dublin and Lübeck and Paris. Yet in Prague it had a poignancy all its own, for there the homelessness of the artist was superimposed upon the estrangement felt by the Jews among gentiles, of German-speaking Jews among Czechs. In souls less shy, subtle, and self-doubting than Kafka's, this tended to produce a pervasive resentment of the outside world as, for instance in the case of his father, an egocentricity devastatingly diagnosed by the son in the never-delivered "Letter to His Father" (1919), the father who, child of a provincial butcher, grew up a Czech and became, after years of hardship, a self-made, quite prosperous businessman in Prague, having changed over to the ruling nation, the Germans, without ever quite mastering their written language: "You were capable . . . of running down the Czechs, and then the Germans, and then the Jews, and . . . not selectively but in every respect, and finally nobody was left except yourself."[1] For the sons, on the

[1] Kafka looked upon himself not as a Kafka but as a Löwy. Among the Löwys, his mother's family, there were many erudite and pious men, even talmudists, and also his favorite uncle, Siegfried Löwy, the "Country Doctor."

other hand, nothing was left but their literature. Their literature was, it seemed to them, their lives and thus their autobiographies. To make things worse, these sons, as Kafka said in a remarkably anti-Semitic letter to Max Brod (June 1921), would enter the German literary language and imagination "boisterously or secretively or even masochistically appropriating foreign capital that they had not earned but, having hurriedly seized it, stolen." In the same letter he said that in the German language only the dialects and the most personal High German are truly alive, while the linguistic middle class is nothing but ashes being made to glow a little by the overagile hands of Jews raking them up. And insofar as the relationship of these Jewish sons to their fathers is concerned, he saw it as a peculiarly Jewish Oedipus complex—and deemed it the occasion and narrowed truth of Freud's theory: "Away from Judaism," this is what these sons, aspiring to the status of German writers, really wanted, but "with their hind legs they remained stuck with the Jewishness of their fathers, while their front legs were unable to find new ground. The despair about this was their inspiration," and this inspiration they held to be their true "reality."[2]

This accounts at least partially for Kafka's unending scruples about publishing what he wrote. But sometimes he was confident that he had succeeded in hammering out that "most personal" German style, which was truly alive; he felt this for the first time after the night of September 22–23, 1912, during which he wrote the story "The Judgment." Indeed, there is not the slightest

[2] Apart from the letters to Milena and Felice, and the undelivered "Letter to His Father," Kafka's correspondence has not yet appeared in English. I quote, in my own translation, from *Briefe 1902–1924*, or from Kurt Wolff, *Briefwechsel eines Verlegers, 1911–63* (Frankfurt am Main: Wolff, 1966).

trace in it of that "stolen" language which occasionally mars what is preserved of his previous writings, for instance "The Description of a Struggle" (1903–04); nothing of the "artistically elated" style of *Der Kunstwart*, a literary magazine dedicated to the cultivation of a "worthy literary idiom" which Kafka regularly read during his student days. "The Judgment" is the "breakthrough" into a form and style entirely his own. It is at the same time—and this is by no means accidental— the outcome of the terror and anxiety caused, as he put it, by "the wound" that "opened" in the long night of the story's composition, the wound the other name of which is father and woman.[3]

2

"The Judgment" is dedicated to Felice Bauer, a woman from Berlin whom Kafka had met on the evening of August 13, 1912, in Prague and to whom soon afterward he began to write ever more urgent love letters, even before he saw her again at Easter 1913. Without becoming his wife, she was twice his fiancée, during the spring of 1914 and for five months beginning in July 1917. Because he believed he loved her, yet did not love her more than his writing, or might have to sacrifice his writing to his love; was unable to be without her; and could not live with her—because of all this, he suffered the agonies of this strangest of love relationships for five years. He made her the heroine in a drama of guilt and punishment that he acted out, then

[3] One day the inescapable computer is likely to discover that "wound" is one of Kafka's most frequent motifs. In the story "A Country Doctor" it is on "the right side, near the hip" of the sick boy, in the place where Adam, before God closed it again, might have had it after the fatal removal of the rib, or Jacob after the divine wrestler had hit him.

and later, with his mind, soul, art, and the sickness of his body, "until finally under the strain of the super-human effort of wanting to marry . . . blood came from the lung," as he wrote in 1919 in the "Letter to His Father." When he first told her that "The Judgment" would be "her" story (October 24, 1912), he also con-fessed that he had refrained with some effort from add-ing to the dedication the words "so that she does not receive presents only from others"; and this addendum, surprisingly enough, he did not suppress out of fear that she might look upon the extraordinary present with horror rather than pleasure. Still, he insisted that there was "not the remotest connection" between her and the story itself except for the fleeting appearance in it of a girl called Frieda Brandenfeld whose name "has the same initials as yours."

Kafka must have known at the time that this was not so, just as there was obviously some playful or tactical untruth in his all but suggesting a little later, in 1913, that the autobiographical allusions had intruded them-selves of their own accord. This laborious dwelling on names, which seems to betray more of his inner state than he would have cared to confess, is so characteristic of Kafka and so revealing of the importance "The Judg-ment" had for him, that it merits to be shown in some detail. On June 2, 1913, he once again wrote to Felice about the story. He discovered only afterward, he said, that Frieda's name had not only the same initials but also the same number of letters as Felice's, while the B in Brandenfeld may have been occasioned not only by *B*auer but also by *B*erlin, the city where she lived, the capital of the Mark *Branden*burg; that *feld* (field) could be closely associated with *Bauer* (farmer); and that Georg Bendemann, the unfortunate hero of the story, was probably given the *mann* merely to supply the poor fellow with a little manly strength for his struggles, while his first name, Georg, had exactly as many letters as Franz, and Bende as many as Kafka (with the vowels in the same places, moreover; Samsa, in "The Metamorphosis," was even better in this regard). Presented with such "discoveries," Felice was bound to doubt that there was, as Kafka claimed, no essential link between her and "her" story; she would have been sure of the link had she known of his diary note of August 14, 1913: "Conclusion for my case from 'The Judgment.' I am indirectly in her debt for the story. But Georg goes to pieces because of his fiancée."

Frieda Brandenfeld's role in "The Judgment" is certainly not slight, although it is true that as a person she hardly comes into view. Yet of all the strenuous attempts Kafka made to explain the story to himself or others, "Georg goes to pieces because of his fiancée" is certainly more convincing than most of the others. Only Kafka's declarations of defeat in his attempts to make sense of the tale may command a first reader's more spontaneous assent: as when, for instance, he called the work "somewhat wild and meaningless," in a letter to Felice (December 4–5, 1912) or when he asked her (June 2, 1913), "Can you discover any meaning in 'The Judgment'—some straightforward, coherent meaning that one could follow? I can't find any, nor can I explain anything in it." Yet again and again he maintained—to Felice, to his publisher, in his diary—that the story was of quite exceptional importance to him. No doubt it is the opening of "the wound" that makes it so.

It is "the wound" that gives the wild, senseless, inconsistent, and inexplicable story that "inner truth" without which it would, as Kafka said, be "nothing"; and there seems to be no doubt that both the wound and the inner truth are also shown in the manner in which

"The Judgment" came to be written. On two occasions, once in a letter to Felice and another time in his diary, Kafka spoke of "birth" in remembering the night that, by "giving" him the "poem," taught him that his efforts to produce a novel were taking place "in the shameful lowlands of writing"; "only *in this way* can writing be done," he said in his diary (September 23, 1912), much as the French symbolists, having learned the doctrine from Poe, believed that only a *brief* poem could be true to the nature of poetic inspiration. "In this way" meant the uninterrupted writing during eight hours of the night; the stiff legs he was scarcely able to move from under the table; "the fearful strain and joy, how the story unfolded before me"; the way it was suddenly possible to express everything because somewhere there burned a fire, consuming and bringing back to life even the strangest thoughts; the blue light of the morning coming through the window; the maid's astonishment as she entered the room and found the bed untouched— "I've been writing until now," Kafka explained. Writing? Indeed, it was rather as if he had been giving birth, as if his body had been torn open along with his soul. If upon reading the story one finds that it has not quite the measure of a genesis thus celebrated, the description may nevertheless serve as supporting evidence for the work's "inner truth" as well as for "the wound" that was its origin.

As Kafka lay in bed during the morning after that night, he thought of things connected with what he had just written: ". . . of course also of my 'The Urban World.' " This is the story he began in February 1911 and soon abandoned.[4] The reader of the fragment cannot help sympathizing with his decision; the beginning

---

[4] It is published in his *Diaries I.*

is unpromising, lacking the kind of vitality that "The Judgment" unquestionably possesses. (A comparison is inevitable because the basic situations are the same: a son, a hostile father, a friend—whom, with schizophrenic playfulness, Kafka named "Franz," a name he would also give to one of the two warders who come to arrest Joseph K. in the opening chapter of *The Trial*—and perhaps a woman waiting in the wings of the as-yet-unwritten, or perhaps not—F. K. had not yet met F. B.) The style of the fragment, although easily recognized as Kafka's, is afflicted with the touch of lameness that bodes ill for its forward movements and makes it difficult to imagine that it could ever negotiate a transition as precarious and decisive as that accomplished in "The Judgment": from realistic narrative to grotesque and absurd nightmare. More than the weight of the story itself, it is Kafka's mastery of this transition, perfect for the first time, that for artistic and not only personal reasons justifies the great importance he attached to "The Judgment." This "going over"—to use the phrase from his meditation "On Parables"—was to occur from then onward on the way not only from the "real" to the dreamlike but also from the commonplace to the embodiments of his metaphysical fantasies. This is the essence of the "Kafkaesque," and is the reason why it is impossible to repeat "in other words" the content of "The Judgment." Of course, "other words" will never do to describe any work of literary rank, but Kafka's works resist the attempt with an obstinacy all their own.

Georg Bendemann, son of an aging and recently widowed businessman, is writing a letter to a bachelor friend who years before had left their common home town to settle in Russia. Considerations of exceptional delicacy have hitherto prevented Georg from telling his friend that a month earlier he had become engaged to a

girl called Frieda Brandenfeld. Now, at last, urged by his
fiancée who is disturbed by Georg's withholding the fact
of their engagement from his friend, he does give him
the news, inviting him at the same time to their wedding. Then he walks across the corridor to his father's
room, apparently to seek his approval of the letter con-
taining the important announcement. It is now that the
transition takes place. What up to this point was an
ordinary and perfectly comprehensible situation suddenly assumes the character of a *danse macabre*, a
sinister *pas de deux* of father and son; this "going over"
is accomplished so effortlessly that in retrospect the
reader may believe he had detected evil specters lurking
in the interstices between the words of the story's first
sentence, short and serene: "It was a Sunday morning
in the very height of spring"; or that the twice-men-
tioned river of the first paragraphs and the bridge had
struck him right away as ominous signals of destiny.
For the story ends with Georg's carrying out the death
sentence passed upon him by his father: he swings
himself over the railings of the bridge and lets himself
drop into the water. He does so voluntarily, if there is
room for the exercise of free will on a scene ruled by
demons—"Georg felt himself urged from the room"—
and while any coroner's findings would be suicide, it is
not for nothing that the father's last words are: "I sentence you now to death by drowning!"

Ignoring much of the preceding "dance," a reader
versed in the mechanics of *Fathers and Sons* (the legacy
left by Turgenev and the Karamazovs to generations of
expressionists and counterculture postexpressionists) or
indeed in the Oedipus patterns of Freud would perhaps
stand his rational ground against this onslaught of the
disturbingly unfamiliar. Kafka himself, on that morning
after, thought not only of his fragmentary "Urban Life"

but also of Freud—a thought that it would have been
hard to avoid even if, at that time, he had already re-
solved, as he did in the "Reflections on Sin, Suffering,
Hope, and the True Way": "Never again psychology!"
Indeed, the Freudian interpreter has never had as good
a time as he enjoys with "The Judgment," and perhaps
he has every right to claim that he knows better than
anyone why Georg observes, "My father is still a giant
of a man" as the sickly old man rises to greet him and
his dressing gown opens while he walks toward the
door. Or why it occurs to the son to offer him his own
bed to lie down in. Or why the father's playing with
Georg's watch chain—he "could not lay him on the bed
for a moment, so firmly did he hang onto the watch
chain"—should give him a feeling all *that* dreadful. Or
why the obscurely (in the original, not so obscurely)
menacing dialogue conducted between the two after the
son had tucked the blankets close about his father—a
dialogue that perhaps a little too emphatically plays on
the double meaning of the German *zudecken* ("cover up
with a blanket," but also "squash," "render powerless"):
"Am I well covered up now?" "So you already find it
snug in bed." "Am I well covered up?" "Don't worry,
you're well covered up."—why this exchange ends with
the father's choleric outburst: having thrown off the
blankets "with a strength that sent them all flying," he
suddenly stands erect on his bed, shouting, "You wanted
to cover me up, but I'm far from being covered up yet!"

On the contrary, the father is vigorously determined
to punish his son. For what? Above all, it would seem,
for his decision to get married from disreputable mo-
tives: " 'Because she lifted up her skirts,' his father
began to flute, 'because she lifted her skirts like this,
the nasty creature,' and mimicking her he lifted his shirt
. . . , 'and in order to make free with her undisturbed

you have disgraced your mother's memory, betrayed your friend, and stuck your father into bed so that he can't move. But he can move, can't he?' " Never before or after, it seems, has Freud ruled so supremely over a piece of literature.

In the "Letter to His Father" that Kafka wrote in 1919, seven years after "The Judgment," he tried to explain to his parent and to himself the nature of their painful feud. Insofar as a letter can say what is in a story, the same themes and more are expressed in simple epistolary prose. Kafka explains how as a child he always felt dwarfed by his father's imposing physical presence of which, at the same time, he was proud; how he was utterly defenseless against his judgments and received every order his father gave as if it were a commandment from Heaven; how he was losing, with regard to the father, all self-confidence, developing instead "a boundless sense of guilt" (here he quotes, not quite accurately, from the last sentence of *The Trial*: "In recollection of this boundlessness I once wrote of someone . . . he is afraid the shame will outlive him," just as before he referred to the conflict as "this terrible trial that is pending between us . . . a trial in which you keep on claiming to be the judge. . . ."); how his "superhuman effort" to break away from the terrifying paternal authority through marrying ended in blood coming from his lung; and how his latest marriage plan—it was in the spring of 1919 when, at the age of thirty-six, he became engaged to a woman whom his father regarded as hopelessly below his station—was met with devastating sarcasm. The revolting parental response to the son's engagement had been amazingly anticipated in "The Judgment." Kafka's father had really reacted to the engagement by saying, "She probably put on a fancy blouse, something those Prague Jewesses

are good at, and right away, of course, you decided to
marry her. And that as fast as possible, in a week,
tomorrow, today. I can't understand you: after all, you're
a grown man, you live in the city, and you don't know
what to do but to marry the next best girl. Isn't there
anything else you can do? If you're frightened, I'll go
with you"—to a brothel, that is.

This, then, would seem to be "the wound" and the
"inner truth" of "The Judgment": a son realizing in the
lucidly recorded sleepless dream of one night his lasting
helplessness in the face of his progenitor's tyrannical
authority, and his incapacity to free himself from the
conviction, instilled or at least caused by his father, that
the sexual act, the power to become a father himself,
is both the corruption of love and a most culpable in-
vasion of the ruler's territory, a belligerent attempt to
"cover him up." As the father, the dominant and therefore proper "owner" of the story, could not possibly be
approached and offended with a dedication, it was given
to the other, weaker partner in the ownership: "her."
As it happened, she was F. B., Felice Bauer or Frieda
Brandenfeld; and it was dedicated to her right at the
beginning of their acquaintance despite—or because of?
—the story's prophesying the doom of their relationship.

Kafka would naturally think of Freud immediately
upon the "birth" of the story. But what about "the dance"
of father and son around the figure of the anonymous
friend who had emigrated to Russia? Kafka's "Letter to
His Father" suggests that his father never showed anything but hostility toward his son's friends, the friend
particularly mentioned being the Yiddish actor Isak
Löwy: "Without knowing him, you compared him . . .
to vermin." Reading this, one cannot help thinking of
the giant insect of "The Metamorphosis." At the same
time one wonders how this fits the "dance" of "The

Judgment," where the father first behaves as if he doubted the very existence of the friend—"Georg, don't deceive me. . . . Do you really have this friend in St. Petersburg?"—then, praising him, declares that he knows him well: "Of course I know your friend. He would have been a son after my own heart." In the same breath he accuses his own son of betraying the friend for this very reason, and finally reveals that he, the father, had long since appropriated the friend and established an *entente cordiale* with him: "But your friend hasn't been betrayed after all. . . . I've been representing him here on the spot."

What is this? What is the point of the father's first pretense of doubt? How, in the father's opinion, has Georg deceived and betrayed his friend? By attaching himself to a woman? By keeping silent about it? The story contains not the slightest hint that the friend might have relied on this kind of faithfulness; on the contrary, the text makes it quite obvious that the correspondence between the friends has been infrequent, and explicitly states that the engagement is only one month old. And although the fiancée previously remarks, "Since your friends are like that, Georg, you shouldn't ever have got engaged at all," in the context "like that" can only mean a lonely and unhappy bachelor friend whom the news of the engagement might cause to feel still more lonely and unhappy or even envious. And is it probable that the father should make himself a kind of *defensor matrimonii* with regard to his son and his friend? Certainly not. It is much more likely that from the depth of Kafka's imagination, filled with fears and anxieties, there rose during that night the diabolic specter of a father who, engaging in a cat-and-mouse game, at first does not want to know his son's friends (in German, the phrase *"von etwas nichts wissen wollen,"* "not to want to know something," implies a determined and hostile refusal to know) and then conspires to isolate his son completely by winning over to his own side one of those on whom the son might have relied for support in the domestic war. The *Letters to Felice*, published long after "The Judgment," may open one's eyes to a feature in Kafka's sketchy portrait of the friend that one had overlooked before: he embodies, without Kafka's himself realizing it, some of the apprehension he felt at that time about his life as a writer—a German-Jewish writer in a Czech land at that: the friend is a stranger among the native inhabitants of the country in which he has come to live, and no less of a stranger in the "colony" that his fellow countrymen have formed there; he resigns himself to becoming a permanent bachelor on account of this social estrangement; his appearance is both sickly and bohemian; his profession is uncertain and unsuccessful; he is, in the eyes of the fiancée, her rival; and above all he is taken away from the son by the father's mysterious conspiracy.

What remains unexplained by all this—and what is probably impervious to explanation—is Kafka's art of writing: this seemingly unimpeded promenading through a jungle as if it were a well-tended garden; this ability to pull all the knots ever tighter with the deceptive gestures of untying them; and this power to plunge the world into darkness by turning on all available lights. Not everyone whose mind is obsessed with a father like Georg Bendemann's writes "The Judgment." This is the all-important fact that many interpreters, not least the psychologists, tend to overlook. However, concerning the shocking tale told by "The Judgment" and the lethal game the father plays with his son, ours is perhaps a more passable inroad into the incomprehensible than even the puzzled and puzzling interpretations that Kafka offered in the diary entry of February 11, 1913, and in the letter to Felice of June 10, 1913, classical examples of *obscurum per obscurius*. Or would Felice have found it helpful to hear that "the story is full of abstractions. . . . The friend is hardly a real person, perhaps he is rather what father and son have in common," that the story itself is a "walk around father and son," with the changeable figure of the friend reflecting "the changing perspective of the relations between father and son"? Although this is simplicity itself compared to the diary exegesis, Felice might not have even tried to understand it, since she is told in the end that Kafka was not at all sure of it himself. Freud, too, would have been left wondering.

3

Whatever is left of the incomprehensible in Kafka after any interpretation rests on a base that is as unshakable as it is difficult of access. This is why his writings, with all their power to perplex, at the same time leave no doubt of their "inner truth"; they are the products of a sensibility which, by the chemistry of its very core, is compelled to reject as invalid the connections between facts and meanings that make for "normalcy" of comprehension. Of course, this is a disposition akin to madness, separated from it only by a writing table, an imagination capable of holding together what appears to have an irresistible tendency to fall apart, and an intelligence of supreme integrity. A father who is not God lifts a finger, and an earthquake ensues. Someone wakes from a dream and *is* what he may have dreamed he was. A dog barks somewhere in the dark, and the chance of intellectual survival is brought into question. "A misunderstanding of some kind; and it will be the ruin of us." "A false alarm on the night bell once answered—it cannot be made good, not ever." An offense invisible to the naked eye causes a volcano of guilt to erupt. Were it not, with Kafka, the source of an extraordinary creativity, this imbalance between occasion and response would indeed be madness, or at least neurosis or hysteria; and if the observer of Kafka's life and work is in a frivolous mood, it may occur to him to call this state of mind *"pavlatche."* *Pavlatche* is a Czech-sounding word of debatable origin, signifying a long balcony that stretches along the court-side of some old Austrian, particularly Prague, houses. This architectural device plays a part in Kafka's account (in the "Letter to His Father") of a childhood episode that he himself deemed very important. One night, the child kept his parents awake by mischievously keeping on crying for water, "partly to be annoying, partly to amuse myself," until his father took him out of bed and onto the *pavlatche*, locking him out there for a while in his nightshirt:

> What was for me a matter of course, that senseless asking for water, and the extraordinary terror of being carried outside were two things that I, my nature being what it was, could never properly connect with each other. Even years afterwards I suffered from the tormenting fancy that the huge man, my father, the ultimate authority, would come almost for no reason at all and take me out of bed in the night and carry me out onto the *pavlatche*, and that meant I was a mere nothing for him.

Paradoxically enough, this may serve as Kafka's own —no doubt arbitrary—causal explanation of how an imaginative world came into being in which the principle of sufficient cause is as good as abolished, above all the rule upon which all justice is founded: that there must be a correspondence between the seriousness of the offense and the degree of the penalty. With Kafka, the offense, far from being an adequate motivation of the punishment, is often not at all recognizable. What, in the first chapter of *Amerika*, is the guilt of the Stoker? And if he is not guilty, it is more likely, to judge by the surrounding circumstances and the removal from the scene of his enthusiastic advocate, young Karl Ross-mann, that "justice" will not be done. Or later in the novel, how almost imperceptible is the offense for which Karl is sent into the American wilderness by his uncle! Or what is the crime of Joseph K. in *The Trial*? Or the wrongdoing, in *The Castle*, for which K. is tormented by an endless sequence of promises and rejections (not to mention the other victims of the Castle's capriciously cruel dispensations)? *Punishments* was to be the name of a volume that Kafka once proposed to his publisher, Kurt Wolff (October 15, 1915); it was to contain, apart from "The Judgment," the two stories "The Metamorphosis" and "In the Penal Colony."

The "legal code," or the moral law underlying these punishments, could hardly be more obscure. "An innocent child, yes, that you were truly, but still more truly have you been a devilish human being!" cries Georg Bendemann's father before he passes the death sentence on his son. Devilish? Nothing in the story could possibly bear out the father's judgment. *Pavlatche*. And if the "metamorphosis" of Gregor Samsa is to be "punishment," as the planned inclusion of "The Metamorphosis" in the volume of that name suggests, then the nature of his guilt is left entirely unilluminated, unless we apply to his life what Tolstoi says of Ivan Ilych's: that his life "had been most simple and most ordinary and therefore most terrible." Kafka of course knew *The Death of Ivan Ilych*.

The third story, "In the Penal Colony," written in the autumn of 1914, three months after Kafka's first engagement to Felice Bauer was broken off, and published as late as 1919, contains the starkest exposition, indeed the "guiding principle," of the terrible incongruity between any possible guilt and a horrible penalty, and this despite the rare fact that here the offense is clearly stated: the soldier who is to die under torture has, by falling asleep, involuntarily disobeyed an order (obviously thought out and given by the kind of sadistically capricious commander who was to acquire notoriety in a later chapter of Europe's nonfictional history). The prisoner is to be executed by a torture machine that the colony's previous commandant had designed, a genius who was at the same time "soldier, judge, mechanic, chemist, and draftsman." This torture machine is so precious and so venerable that the officer meticulously cleans his hands before showing a drawing of it to the witness of the impending execution, an explorer who has voyaged to the colony. (What terrifyingly precise prophecy, this cleanliness of an executioner who is convinced of the venerability of the institution and its administration of "justice"!) In the course of its slow killing, this machine deeply engraves the sentence into the victim's body. And as the witness asks whether the condemned man knows his sentence, he learns that he does not: "There would be no point in telling him. He'll learn it on his body." (The German original alludes to the idiom *"etwas am eigenen Leib zu spüren bekommen"*—"to come to experience something on one's own body." Once again Kafka takes a figurative saying literally, and reveals the horror underlying not only this particular phrase but, as it were, the world itself.) "But surely he knows that he has been sentenced?" the explorer inquires. "Not that either." And when the witness incredulously insists, "But he must have had some chance of defending himself," he not only is told that this is not the case but also is informed of "the guiding principle" that rules the legal system in which judge and executioner are one and the same person: "Guilt is never to be doubted."

"Guilt is never to be doubted." Surely this suggests the doctrine of original sin, of universal guilt—and indeed Kafka suspected that he understood the Fall of Man better than anyone. Again and again he was driven to speculate about the meaning of the guilt that God's first children incurred through disobeying Him. But while guilt is never to be doubted, God is very much in doubt. The existence of the Law is never in question, even if its text is or has become illegible. Only in the six hours of his terrible dying does the prisoner in the penal colony begin to decipher the judgment that, presumably, has been passed on him in the name of the Law. Yet even then he reads it not with his eyes but "with his wounds," and by that time the machine "has pierced him quite through and casts him into the pit. . . . The judgment has been fulfilled and we . . . bury him." But what exactly *is* the Law upon which the judgment is founded? And who—in the name of whom? —is the law giver? Is it, in the penal colony, the commandant, who is already "soldier, judge, mechanic, chemist, and draftsman," a parody of God, a god, however, unable to prevent the final destruction of his machine? Or is He, in "The Metamorphosis," represented by the simple vitality that "in spite of all the sorrow of recent times" and all the insect trouble suffered by the family, allows Gregor Samsa's sister in the end to blossom into an attractive young woman ready to find a husband and bring forth healthy children? Or, in "The Judgment," is it the father, pronouncing the sentence of death upon his "devilish" son? Or, in *Amerika*, is it the incongruously offended uncle who punishes his nephew? Or, in *The Trial* and *The Castle*, is it the unapproachable and invisible authority that condemns, torments, or executes its appointed culprits? And why, if it is a matter of *universal* guilt, does it fall to the lot of an undistinguished son to play the role of the sacrificial lamb? Why is it an ordinary commercial traveler, or an all but anonymous land surveyor, who must carry upon his shoulders the sins of the world?

There is no answer to any of these questions; indeed, there is no *answerable* question to be found anywhere in the works of Kafka. For it is in the nature of his questions that they allow of no answers: in the unfinished story "Investigations of a Dog," the "investigator" says of himself that, like every other dog, he has the impulse to question as well as the simultaneous impulse "not to answer." It is even true to say that Kafka's questions are not only unanswerable but also unquestionable. This is one of the secrets of his art: he wields the magic by which to remove the question mark from the questionable. Where he succeeds, the questions have been transformed into an indisputable givenness, something as affirmative as trees or mountains or oceans or odradeks.

Who is Odradek? A plaything *de profundis*, "hero" of the little story "The Cares of a Family Man" (1917), an absurdity with a name that nobody appears to have given it and that makes no sense. ("Some say the word Odradek is of Slavonic origin and try to account for it on that basis. Others again believe it to be of German origin, only influenced by Slavonic. The uncertainty of both interpretations allows one to assume with justice that neither is accurate, especially as neither of them provides an intelligent meaning of the word." However, the Czech verb *odraditi* does mean something: to advise against. If Kafka meant to allude to it in "Odradek," he must have done so—alas, in vain—as a warning to interpreters.) Odradek looks like a star-shaped spool and does seem to have thread wound upon it, but the spool is as useless as its thread, old, short bits of varied sorts and colors, badly tangled up. Nor is it just a spool, for by a device that a child at play might have invented, it stands upright "as if on two legs"; it looks senseless but "in its own way perfectly finished"; it nimbly runs and climbs about and can never be caught and examined, and when it admits to having no fixed address, it even laughs its lungless laughter that sounds "like the rustling of fallen leaves." Without ever discovering an answer, the worried family father tries to search out its nature and purpose. True, it apparently does no harm, but neither is it of any use, and to think that it may even survive him is "almost painful" to him who cares for order in the affairs of his house. The story of Odradek, were it not also darkly oppressive, would be Kafka's entirely humorous parable of that question-that-is-no-question but is a specimen of the absurdity of existence. Odradek derives its unquestionable—and unquestionably absurd—existence from a world which despite its teeming with inescapable cares and compelling problems has no lungs for answers. Paul Klee could have painted Odradek, and Charlie Chaplin, giving up for a little while his role as the homeless tramp, might have played the family man who, with an expressionless face and yet desperately, pursues the mystery of the agile little creature.

There are many examples of this in Kafka's works:

the blue-striped celluloid balls with the rattling interior sounds, ideal toys for children but exasperating to the elderly bachelor Blumfeld (another part for Chaplin) as they relentlessly follow him, jumping up and down and, in their duality, apparently obeying some unknown law that makes it a punishable offense to remain alone and a bachelor like Blumfeld or the author himself. Or the coal bucket, so light with emptiness that it carries the destitute and freezing Bucket Rider through the air to the overheated house of the coal dealer, there in vain to beg for coal—a magical flying bucket out of a child's dream, which is at the same time heavy with the un-. answerable question why the world is so cold and so pitilessly unjust.

The Law without a lawgiver, original sin without a god to sin against: this is the essence of the negative theology that pervades Kafka's stories and novels. The protagonists are sinful almost *because* there is no God to disobey, guilty almost *because* there is no Sinai, for although there is no God and no lawgiver, their souls are cast in the mold in which the fear of God and obedience to His laws is inscribed. Sin and guilt more often than not appear to lie not in any *doing*, but in *being*, in being a separate individual, or, to use Schopenhauer's terms, in the *principium individuationis* itself —an unprincipled *principium individuationis*, as it were, for it is only individual sons and not the individual fathers and friends, only the Gregor Samsas and not the parents, sisters, or lodgers, only the K.'s and not the other citizens in their towns or villages who are fatally affected by the principle's machinations. And it is with the K.'s in their towns and villages that the pains of individuation are no doubt accentuated by Kafka's Jewishness, by the liberated and yet spiritually continued ghetto existence of the German-speaking Jews in Prague. The *principium individuationis* is, it would seem, with Kafka the ultimate cause of the wound that opened during that night when a son desired to assert his own individual will against the authority of an older and greater will, sickly and yet powerfully represented by the father, and wrote "The Judgment."

Coming upon the drama of individuation, a student of German philosophy or at least of those philosophers who played a role in Kafka's intellectual education, cannot help thinking of Schopenhauer.[5] Schopenhauer was the consummate dramatist of the universal Will, the life-force of undifferentiated totality, splitting up into innumerable entities, tigers and lambs, Cains and Abels, killing one another or senselessly propagating their own species on behalf of that universal Will that animates them all. Schopenhauer ceaselessly insisted upon the "godless" sin of the individual's breaking away from the not yet individualized totality—and for Schopenhauer the individual *is* this breaking away—and upon its necessarily tragic and only rarely joyous self-assertion; and Schopenhauer wrote about this in a prose so beautiful that the aesthetic reader, utterly against the intention of the pessimistic philosopher, may fall in love with an "individualized" world that has brought forth so ex-

[5] The first philosophical conversation between Kafka and Max Brod, the "founding" conversation of their friendship, appears to have taken place, according to Brod's Kafka biography, after a lecture on Schopenhauer, given by Brod in 1902 to a German academic club in Prague, and although Kafka may never have studied Schopenhauer systematically, this philosopher was—not least through Max Brod—very much present in the intellectual atmosphere in which he grew up. Schopenhauer's *Collected Works* were among the books that Kafka owned.

quisite a philosophical writer. Has not this ambiguity some bearing on Kafka's endless oscillations between passionately seeking the "selfless" life of writing (as a "form of prayer") and then again condemning literature as a diabolical service to his vanity, that ugly manifestation of the self-will? This ambiguity, the very burden of his relationship with Felice, is only part of an even greater one: his denying the spiritual justification of any individual existence or its propagation through the sexual act, and, on the other hand, his celebrating as the "good life" the individual's self-realization. (More of this contradiction will be said in discussing Kafka's marriage plans, and above all the lucid madness of *The Trial.*) And although no writer has been more plagued than Kafka by such an irreconcilable and extreme polarity,[6] it is yet true to say that the first and fundamental design of "The Judgment" or "The Metamorphosis" or "In the Penal Colony" is unequivocally Schopenhauerian: to be an individual is a culpable encroachment upon the peace of nonbeing, or at least of not being an individual. "Those who curse life and therefore think not being is the greatest or the sole nondeceptive happiness, must be right," says Kafka in the Fragments contained in the volume *Dearest Father*; and this is only one of a great number of his aphorisms that read like marginal glosses on a text by Schopenhauer. Schopenhauer seems to be the prompter of many of Kafka's lines, indeed of the whole *Trial*, when at the end of Chapter VIII of his

[6] Thomas Mann, no stranger to it (or, for that matter, to Schopenhauer), attracted Kafka's sympathy and deep interest by his ability—it is to be surmised—to resolve in most of his works a similar, if less consuming, tension through his humanely conciliatory irony. In this respect and by comparison, Kafka's irony is deadly.

Miscellaneous but Systematically Ordered Thoughts about Many Subjects he implicitly denies the need for a Last Judgment on the grounds that the world, as it is and continues to be, is quite enough of a judgment passed on all those who exist in it.

Where deliverance from the *principium individuationis* is near, and be it in the most cruel circumstances, there often appears in Kafka's works the reflection of a transcendent light on the faces of those about to be freed from their guilty individual state. While Schopenhauer is fond of thus interpreting the peace that shows in the features of the dead, with Kafka it sometimes seems that the lifting of the curse of individuation is welcomed ecstatically, that the victim himself rejoices in the fulfillment of the Law exacting the supreme penalty for the sin against the original all-oneness. It is as if many a terrible dying described by Kafka were perverse love-deaths, partaking of the raptures of a final reunion after the sorrows of a long deprivation. This is how in the penal colony, for example, the officer-executioner describes the face of the condemned when "the Harrow," writing the judgment into his flesh, pierces his body: "But how quiet he grows at just about the sixth hour. Enlightenment comes to the most dull-witted. It begins around the eyes. From there it radiates. A moment that might tempt one to get under the Harrow oneself." Even if it is a negative ecstasy, it is yet ecstasy; and although the passage, like numerous others in Kafka's works, reads as if it had been inspired not as much by Schopenhauer as by the Marquis de Sade (of whom Kafka, as Gustav Janouch reports, said that he was "the true patron of our age"), it might have been once again upon the instruction of Schopenhauer himself that the face of the officer who eventually does "get under the Harrow" himself, desperate as he is at the prospect of the stern Law, together with the ingenious machine that serves it, being abolished by the world, shows no sign of the "promised redemption." "What the others had found in the machine the officer had not found." Upon the instruction of Schopenhauer: for the philosopher abhorred suicide as a means of overcoming individual existence, seeing it not as self-conquest but, on the contrary, as a desperate, hysterical, and perverse self-assertion—the precise characterization of the officer's self-execution.

Even in *The Trial*, where Joseph K. suffers a death of unrelieved shame, all those who stand accused and in all probability will be sentenced to death, are beautiful, as the Lawyer explains, meaning that they have *become* beautiful "in the process" of their having been drawn into the net of the Law (process = *Prozess* = trial); and the beauty they have thus acquired seems to mark a stage on the journey beyond the principle of individuation, inviting as it does the self-abandonment of the eruptive, impersonal "unindividualized" sexual relations between Joseph K. and Leni, the Lawyer's maid. And *Amerika*—Kafka's first attempted novel and one which, to judge by the fragment that exists, would certainly not have resisted a happy ending—was meant to issue in the great utopia of "The Nature Theatre of Oklahoma," where "everyone is welcome" to take part in the vast all-embracing play of the world. In the "almost limitless" spaces of this theater, the self, having suffered the pains of division and isolation, would be most joyously and "as if by some celestial witchery" received again into the unity from which it had been separated. This was Kafka's plan, according to Max Brod's report in the Postscript. Karl Rossmann, young,

innocent, charming—early and happy toy of Kafka's
epic imagination before his other K.'s were conceived in
a tragic key—was to enter the paradise that would
redeemingly restore its true "in" to the *"dividuum"*—to
use Nietzsche's very Schopenhauerian etymology of the
word "individual" (VIII, 75).

No paradise awaits Georg Bendemann at the end of
"The Judgment." Yet this story, too, ends with the return
of a guiltlessly guilty individual to the fluid, unformed,
as it were prenatal element. Commanded to cease exist-
ing as an individual for the offense of having begun to
assert his selfhood: this is all that can be said with certainty about the meaning, within the story, of guilt and
punishment; and the pitiless irony of Georg's last words
—"Dear parents, I have always loved you, all the same"
(father and mother and no mention of his fiancée)—
reveal how close he has remained to his beginning, the
"mistake" of which is being made good at the fatal moment when he lets himself drop into the river. This is
no far-fetched speculation. In the diary attempt to il-
lumine and thus perhaps to lay the ghost of that night
(February 11, 1913), Kafka himself remarked that the
fiancée, not yet having become his wife, has remained
outside the bloodstream uniting father and son, and is
therefore easily driven off by the father, the guardian,
so to speak, of a community more powerful than the
individual and certainly the personified denial of the
son's selfhood. The surrender of individuality in death
is related to that of Eros and sex, at least for the romantic and postromantic sensibility, formed within the
orbit of Schopenhauer, Wagner, and Freud, and Max
Brod's memory is probably reliable when he reports
Kafka as saying that, writing the last sentence of "The
Judgment," he thought of a powerful sexual sensation,

"a strong ejaculation."[7] In its crude way, it confirms that "The Judgment" is in the last resolve about the *principium individuationis* and the horrors attendant upon its conquest through what Kafka himself called "a false death"—horrors as perversely ecstatic as the radiance of redemption on the faces of victims "In the Penal Colony."

4

The form of art which, according to Schopenhauer's *World as Will and Idea*, is at the furthest remove from the *principium individuationis* is music; music is the voice of the universal Will itself, the sound of the metaphysical essence of the world. For Schopenhauer, it is capable of conveying the memory of a blissfully undivided state of being, or of anticipating the harmony that will ensue upon the individual's victory over the self-will and thus over himself, a conquest that would "correct the mistake" and restore the peace and integrity of the all-oneness. Music in Kafka's work is almost always related to this Schopenhauerian doctrine. This is the more remarkable as Kafka was not musical in the sense of having any special musical gift or understanding. Despite having been introduced in his childhood to the piano and violin, he played no instrument as an adult. After having been to a concert devoted to Brahms, he observed in his diary (December 13, 1911) that he was unable—and this he called the essence of his lack of musicality—to enjoy a piece of music connectedly: "Only now and then it evokes a response in me, and

---

[7] The point is lost in the translation of the last sentence: "At this moment an unending stream of traffic was just going over the bridge." The German for "traffic" is *Verkehr*. Its connotations are the same as those of "intercourse."

how rarely is this a musical one." (The travel diary of the following year records a garden concert in Weimar [July 3, 1912]. He was "entirely captivated" by the music of *Carmen*, the opera of the French love-death, which Nietzsche pugnaciously declared superior to the German-Wagnerian one; besides, Kafka had just then fallen in love with a travel acquaintance.)

Despite Kafka's unmusical disposition, music—or at least a kindred sensation of sound—is in his works always the harbinger of great things. Listening to music, souls that are imprisoned in their individuations may have a premonition of the true sustenance inaccessible to them in their individualized lives. When, for instance, Gregor Samsa, transformed into a giant insect, intently listens to his sister playing the violin, while the lodgers, despite her playing "so beautifully," appear to be only irritated, Gregor's degraded and repulsive shape would almost seem to be a perversely conceived superior distinction. No one is able to appreciate music as much as he: only he feels that it is "opening before him . . . the way to the unknown nourishment he craved"—the same kind of nourishment which, in a later story, might have saved the Hunger Artist from having to starve himself to death: he says he *had* to fast because he couldn't find the food that suited him.[8]

In a posthumously published sketch by Kafka which, although it has appeared independently under the title "Advocates," was clearly a short rehearsal for *The Trial*, the "I" (it is written in the first person) wonders whether

---

[8] The English translators of "The Metamorphosis" made a rather grievous mistake in rendering the German *"War er ein Tier, da ihn Musik so ergriff?"* by "Was he an animal that music had such an effect upon him?" The meaning of the sentence is: "As music moved him so deeply, was he [really] an animal?"

he is under judgment before a law court. He probably is, he thinks, for he can hear "a droning noise" which comes incessantly from a distance and fills "every room to such an extent that one had to assume it came from everywhere, or, what seemed more likely, that just the place where one happened to be standing was the very place where the droning originated." The "I" hearing the "music" of the Law is obviously identical with the Joseph K. of *The Trial* who, when he is shown the strange "Offices" of the Court and almost faints in the oppressive air of that attic, suddenly cannot understand what the officials individually say to him; what he hears is a din that fills the whole place and is pierced by a steady high note, like a siren's. And in *The Castle* it is not *one* voice that is heard on the village telephones when they are connected with the high seat of authority, but a sound more like a choral humming; *all* officials up there are perpetually telephoning, and it is this *collective* talk that the village receives. Yet it is not mere humming, but a sound of a peculiar kind; it seems to require a more profound hearing than ordinary ears are capable of, or, as the village representative explains to K., "This humming and singing transmitted by our telephones is the only real and reliable thing you'll hear, everything else is deceptive" (V). Because every particular voice is fallacious, in its particularity incapable of speaking the truth, what counts is the sound or music of some transcendent universality, of something that has not yet been articulated or divided into single forms: these, in any case, would easily be pierced by that unchangeable note of the siren which in Kafka's imagination seems to be like a trumpet of the Last Judgment announcing the abolition of the *principium individuationis*.

But it is "Investigations of a Dog," a story Kafka

wrote at the time of "The Hunger Artist," that is, in a strikingly Schopenhauerian sense, his most "musical." He left it unfinished, and although, had he completed it, he might have tightened it and eliminated its meandering long-windedness, it is obvious why it was so hard for him to bring it to a conclusion. It begins with the dog's recalling "the time when I was still a member of the canine community, sharing in all its preoccupations, a dog among dogs," and it ends with: "Freedom! Certainly such freedom as is possible today is a wretched business. But nevertheless freedom. . . ." Clearly, this freedom would have to be such as to liberate the dog finally from his membership in the canine community and recover the condition before dogs became "as doggish as today," before they paid with excessive doggishness for their first fathers' "aberration," their straying from a state when the true Word "was there, was very near at least, on the tip of everybody's tongue." However, the excuse of these remote forefathers may well have been that in sinning they could hardly have had a notion that their sin

> was to be an endless one, they could still literally see the crossroads, it seemed an easy matter to turn back whenever they pleased, and if they hesitated to turn back it was merely because they wanted to enjoy a dog's life for a little while longer; it was not yet a genuine dog's life, and already it seemed intoxicatingly beautiful to them, so what must it become in a little while, a very little while, and so they strayed farther. They did not know what we can now guess at, contemplating the course of history: that change begins in the soul before it appears in ordinary existence, and that, when they began to enjoy a dog's life, they must already have possessed real old dogs' souls, and were by no means so near their starting point as

they thought or as their eyes feasting on all dog-gish joys tried to persuade them.

This is Kafka's humorous version of the Fall and of an original sin that lies in the creature's insistence upon "enjoying a dog's life," upon being in one's body what one had already become in one's soul. And if the particular dog of Kafka's story was to achieve in the end the surpassing liberation from the fetters of its dog-hood, Kafka would have had to succeed in describing the absolute freedom that lies beyond a world of merely "wretched" freedoms, the blissful freedom that existed before the *principium individuationis* held sway and will be again after all separateness has been tran-scended. No writer has ever accomplished this, not even the divine author of Genesis who, speaking of the prelapsarian state of affairs, incongruously spoke of "Adam" and "Eve." But—*pace* Milton's license—there could not possibly have been any particular man or particular woman before "Adam knew Eve his wife." For an Adam who did not desire his Eve would not yet be Adam, and an Eve, before falling for the serpent's advice to seduce him, would not yet be Eve. Neither was Isaiah more successful when in his ecstasy he prophesied that, upon the regaining of Paradise, "the wolf . . . shall dwell with the lamb, and the leopard shall lie down with the kid. . . ." Speaking in this way, he overlooked the undeniable fact that no *real* wolves, lambs, leopards, and kids could enter into such pacific arrangements: they would have to cease being what they are. A wolf that does not feed on lambs is no wolf —any more than a dog, having remedied the "funda-mental error" of its forefathers by stepping out of "the canine community," would still be a dog.

This failure which Kafka shares with Genesis and

Isaiah is unavoidable: it is due to the limitation of language itself. For language with its nouns and verbs and particularizing adjectives is the idiom of the *principium individuationis*; and, indeed, how is one to describe a dog that is no longer a dog? It was with good reason that Schopenhauer allowed only music, not language, to reach beyond that principle and convey speechless, limitless universality; and nothing could be more Schopenhauerian than "that concert" through which the chosen dog of Kafka's story was to discover his true mission. He had long lived in the dark, distinguished from his fellow dogs only by some sense of "discrepancy, some little maladjustment causing a slight feeling of discomfort" that was yet like "a premonition of great things." But then came "that concert"; and the dog knew that it had fallen to his lot endlessly to question his existence—even if his impulse to question was almost as strong as the impulse not to answer—to search and finally perhaps to achieve the unlimited freedom that essentially consisted in being free of himself, indeed free of any self. The concert was given by seven dogs— seven: a mystical number—of which one could not even be quite sure whether they were real dogs or conjured up by the imagination of the listener "out of some place of darkness, to the accompaniment of terrible sounds such as I had never heard before. . . . But it is too much to say that I even saw them. . . . I inwardly greeted them as dogs . . . although I was profoundly confused by the sounds that accompanied them." Like all recorded mystical initiations, this, too, exceeded the initiate's power of comprehension, and if the artistry of these musician dogs was beyond belief, the miracle that they themselves should endure their own music without being destroyed by it was even more shattering. Even the listener dog is literally beside himself, losing his sense of time and space, invariable dimensions of individuation. In trying to convey what this victim of transcendence experiences, Kafka comes close to conjuring up a state of being in which the individual is truly beyond individuation:

> The music gradually got the upper hand, literally knocked the breath out of me and swept me away from those actual little dogs, and quite against my will, while I howled as if some pain were being inflicted upon me, my mind could attend to nothing but this blast of music which seemed to come from all sides, from the heights, from the deeps, from everywhere, surrounding the listener, overwhelming him, crushing him, and over his swooning body still blowing fanfares so near that they seemed far away and almost inaudible. . . . It robbed me of my wits, whirled me around in its circles as if I myself were one of the musicians instead of being only their victim, cast me hither and thither, no matter how much I begged for mercy. . . .

The Biblical narrator says of Adam and Eve in the Garden that they were naked and were not ashamed. Shame they felt only when, having tasted the fruit from the Tree of Knowledge, they "knew" each other as the two individuals Adam and Eve. And as if to hint at the place whence the dog musicians hailed—some Eden that lies on the other side of the *principium individuationis* —Kafka says of them that shame, the irrepressible companion of individuation, was unknown to them. They violated the law governing the conduct of all dog individuals: "They had flung away all shame, the wretched creatures were doing the very thing which is both most ridiculous and indecent in our eyes; they were walking on their hind legs. Fie on them! They were uncovering

their nakedness, blatantly making a show of their nakedness." What is more (if it is not the same), they seemed
altogether incapable of noticing the presence of other
dogs and never responded when one of them addressed
them. "Incredible! Incredible!" exclaims the investigating dog, for this is, among dogs, so terrible an offense
against good manners that he who has been thus in-
sulted comes to doubt whether these musicians were
what they seemed: dogs. The investigating dog resolves
to enlighten them, indeed to castigate them for their
abominable conduct; he might even have succeeded
had the music not taken possession of him once more:
"a clear piercing, continuous note which came . . .
from the remotest distance—perhaps the real melody
in the midst of the music" that forced him to his knees.
"Besides, it was not long before the dogs vanished with
all their music and their radiance into the darkness
from which they had emerged." The piercing note again!
This time it is the last word, as it were, of the musician
dogs.

One can hardly go further, within the limits of the
language of individuation, in alluding to a condition
that is the suspense of individuation, the correction of
the "decisive, the fundamental error that I must surely
have made," as the questioning dog suspects. For what
he seeks is that "ultimate science," the science of freedom, which is unattainable so long as dogs are doggish:
individuals are shut off from "the true Word." The dog
of the "Investigations" is at times prepared to fast himself to extinction for such a science. For individuation
is that mysterious and utterly incongruous dispensation
that has left the "impossible" desire in the soul of the
individual, a craving not appeasable in this individualized world, a hunger to which this world does not cater
with the proper nourishment. If, says the dog, I "were

unable by the diligent labor of a long life to achieve my desire, that would prove that my desire is impossible, and complete hopelessness must follow." This is Kafka's foremost theme, his song of "absurdity": the impossible desire to be liberated from guilt, a desire which—after all is said and done about condemned sons, meta-morphosized salesmen, exiled nephews, accused bank clerks, unwelcome land surveyors, hunger artists, or investigating dogs—ultimately aims at the transcend-ence of individuation itself.[9]

[9] If this seems too portentous a way of taking leave of one of Kafka's most humorous works, it should not be forgotten that even his humor is tinged with spiritual gravity and dis-tress, and that even his seemingly light and cheerful play-things are purchased in the deep. Nowhere is this—some-times very disquieting—vicinity of the mind's abysses and its aesthetic plays more apparent than in a letter Kafka wrote to Kurt Wolff in November 1918 about "In the Penal Colony." He emphatically demands that after the paragraph conclud-ing with "iron spike" there should be some empty space left, "marked by asterisks or in some other way." The paragraph in question, which ends: ". . . through the forehead went the point of the great iron spike," concludes the description of the officer's self-execution, and it is one of the most terrifying passages in Kafka's works. But at this point Kafka's greatest concern was the look of the printed page. In "Investigations," the scientific interest of the dog centers upon the origins of canine food: Is it produced by the earth or does it come from above? Certainly, the earth does supply it, as long as dogs keep the rule "Water the ground as much as you can" (which, anyway, they do compulsively), and yet the dog believes he has found in his scientific researches "that the main part of the food that is discovered on the ground . . . comes from above; indeed customarily we snap up most of our food . . . before it has reached the ground at all." Of course, Kafka's comic invention, often solemnly overlooked by interpreters, is that man is invisible to the dogs of the story, so that the food he throws to them or dangles above their heads, inciting them to perform "ritual dances and incantations in order to obtain it," to them ap-pears to come from Heaven. Although Kafka has a great deal of theological fun with this invention, it is at the same time

Although the guilt that lies in being an individual is, with Kafka, the *ultimate* justification of all punishments, it would be naïve to believe that this almost theological sin explains all his obscurities. At best it illumines the innermost chamber of the edifice, but the surrounding labyrinth remains. In its twisted architecture there still lurks, among others, the question: what is the specific guilt of the culprits, and what is the specific law in the name of which they are sentenced? Despite one's awareness of the ultimate sin, it is impossible to suppress such questions. They are inevitable; and if the inevitable is also the legitimate, they are legitimate questions, even if Kafka's art is such that it deprives them of their self-confidence; for the labyrinth not only houses the questions but is filled with those mysteriously transparent vapors of senselessness that all but choke them. Still, the questions survive simply because the stories are stories and are therefore about individuals who live among other individuals, differing from them by their particular destinies and guilts, and what is true of "The Judgment," "The Metamorphosis," *The Trial*, and *The Castle* is certainly true in a much more complicated

---

pervaded by profound seriousness. The same is true of the *"Lufthunde,"* the little lapdogs that, resting on the laps of their invisible mistresses, seem to float in the air. In describing them, Kafka never deviates from his "fantastic realism": there is not a single feature or move of these hovering creatures that could not be that of lapdogs minus their human support. "They have no relation whatever to the general life of the community, they hover in the air, and that is all, and life goes on in its usual way; someone now and then refers to art and artists, but there it ends." The comedy as well as the seriousness of this is enhanced by Kafka's using the word *"Lufthunde,"* a variation upon the Marxian term *"Luftmenschen,"* human beings that are "up in the air" insofar as they have no necessary or even clearly defined function in the social economy. This, he always believed, was true of himself as a writer.

way of "In the Penal Colony." The complication is not that the guilt, although clearly defined, is so horribly outdistanced by the punishment that it amounts to no definable guilt whatever; it lies rather in the insinuation that the law behind the lethal torture of the condemned is at least as justified as the leniency of the more "humane" new commandant; that the old order, confusingly allied to the newest technology and automation—"Up till now a few things [in the machine] still had to be set by hand, but from this moment it works all by itself"—evokes a faith that the faithful believe is worth dying for, while the convictions of the liberal visitor are not even strong enough for him to help soldier and condemned man to escape from the abominable penal colony. "It's always a ticklish matter to intervene decisively in other people's affairs," he says to himself.

It is this unresolvable ambivalence that the penal colony has in common not only with "The Judgment" but above all with *The Trial* which Kafka began at about the same time (autumn 1914) and never completed. Kafka's imagination, indissolubly wedded to his intelligence, was helplessly attracted by the Law without being able to form a clear idea of it, such as would be the condition of uninhibited moral judgments, the condition too of any sensible administration of justice beyond—or before—the acknowledgment of that universal guilt which arises from individuation itself. As the nature of the light reveals itself to the moth that circles it with insatiable curiosity only by burning the moth in the end, so for Kafka the sole proof of the Law was in the indisputable punishment it exacted from him. Therefore he was unable to sustain any particular indictments against anyone except himself—and even not quite against himself. The "Letter to His Father" comes closest to being an accusation of another, but even this document is imbued with a sense of guilt that is in "being" rather than in "doing," in an unfathomable dispensation of nature rather than in misdeeds. At the end of the "Letter," or almost at the end, as if he was writing a drama, he allows his father to speak in his own defense, indeed to counterattack, and this in so subtly intelligent a manner as would have exceeded the father's intellectual gifts: "At first," says the father, speaking a text invented by the son, "you repudiate . . . all guilt and responsibility; in this our methods are the same. But whereas I then attribute the sole guilt to you as frankly as I mean it"—for the father believes that he *does* know the Law, and with unbroken spontaneity distinguishes what he takes to be right from wrong—"you want to be 'overly clever' and 'overly affectionate' at the same time and acquit me of all guilt." Yet it only *seems* so: in truth, it is the son's most clever ruse. What can be read between the lines of his letter, despite all the niceties about "character and nature and helplessness," is that actually "I [the father] have been the aggressor while everything you were up to was self-defense." By this most sophisticated method—and this the playwright son writes into the part of his father—the son has shown not only that he is himself without guilt but that, on the contrary, all the guilt is with the father. Nonetheless the son, the innocent, is willing to forgive and most magnanimously suggests that in the final resolve the father, too, is without guilt.

The father, according to the brief of his son, his most able advocate, admits that they fight with each other; but, he says, there are two kinds of combat: one is "the chivalrous combat in which independent opponents pit their strength against each other. . . . And there is the combat of vermin, which not only sting but, on top of it, suck your blood in order to sustain their own life." This, of course, rises from the same depths of the wounded mind as did seven years before Gregor Samsa's metamorphosis[10] and, linked to it, the ever-present and guilt-ridden thought of the inability to marry. It is certainly no accident that this, in the imagined words of the father, makes for the finale of the letter:

> . . . when you recently wanted to marry, you wanted . . . at the same time not to marry, but in order not to have to exert yourself you wanted me to help you with this non-marrying by forbidding this marriage. . . . I did not dream of it. . . . But did the self-restraint with which I left the marriage up to you do me any good? Not in the least. My aversion to your marriage would not have prevented it; on the contrary, it would have been an added incentive for you to marry the girl, for it would have made the "attempt at escape," as you put it, complete. And my consent to your marriage did not prevent your reproaches, for you prove that I am in any case to blame for your not marrying. . . . If I am not very much mistaken, you are preying on me even with this letter itself.

The part of the father is endowed with at least as much inner conviction as is the part that the son delivers in his own person. It is the art of a truly dramatic writer that has gone into this letter: whoever it is that holds the stage at any particular moment is in the right. And the final truth—if this situation permits of such—is

[10] Was the wounded mind helped in this by a passage, near the beginning, in Dostoevski's *Notes from the Underground*: "I wish to tell you, gentlemen . . . why I have never even been able to become an insect. . . . I solemnly declare to you that I have often wished to become an insect, but could never attain my desire"? Kafka's diaries as well as his library show that he was, of course, a reader of Dostoevski.

contained in the words with which the son begins his last reply to the father: "My answer to this is that, after all, this whole rejoinder . . . does not come from you, but from me"; the son, that is, being in control of the whole epistolary scene, might have suppressed this ultimate touch of moral inconclusiveness. But it only seems that he had this choice. The truth is that he couldn't help writing as he did. For this fanatically honest writer —always ready to suspect himself of dishonesty (and only very rarely right in doing so, unless we conclude that his kind of self-consciousness renders "honesty" impossible)—was quite unable to reverse "The Judgment" and wholly to condemn his father, as unable as he was unequivocally to define guilt in "The Judgment" and "The Metamorphosis"; or to take sides in the struggle between cruel orthodoxy and vague liberality in the "Penal Colony"; or even to hint at an unrestrained disapproval of the dissolute guardians of the Law in *The Trial*; or to arbitrate between the claims of the Hunger Artist and those of the young panther; or even, in his own case, to make up his mind whether he should marry or else remain an ascetically dedicated bachelor writer—the terrible indecision that is the burden of the *Letters to Felice*.

Marriage or Literature? The *Letters to Felice*

I

"When you recently wanted to marry, you wanted . . .. at the same time not to marry," says the father concerning his son's marriage plans, according to the dramatization of the son. The man who had written the letters to Felice Bauer knew only too well that this was abysmally true. Had Max Brod known that "invention" from "Letter to His Father" when he disobeyed his closest friend's last will and published what Kafka apparently wanted him to destroy, he could have taken his cue from it in justifying his decision. For the demon of ambivalence haunted Kafka as much with regard to his writings as it did in his relationship with his fiancée: "When you wanted me to burn your manuscripts, you wanted me at the same time to publish them," is what Max Brod might have said.

The heroine of Kafka's last story, the singing mouse Josephine, knows this state of mind. She has only one desire: to win "the public, unambiguous, permanent recognition of her art"; in order to reach her goal, she one day perversely refuses to sing any more. Indeed, she disappears altogether, so that people must search for her and fiercely entreat her to give concerts again. "What Josephine really wants is not what she puts into words." What she puts into words (and deeds) is those *"Winkelzüge,"* shifts and crooked moves, of which Kafka speaks with his customary moral exaggeration in a letter to Max Brod of June 26, 1922—another document Max Brod might have drawn upon in his defense—where he writes of the calculations that go into his own dismissals of his literary achievements: yes, partly he *means* the negative estimates which so frequently accompany his stories on their way to the publisher, but to a large extent they are designed to make it impossible for the publisher to concur with them.

Kafka's ambivalence toward his writings is only the other side of a tortured inability to be integrated into what enviously he looked upon as "life": a vocation more satisfactory to the soul than his legal-clerical work, a dedication more peaceful and "natural" than the hungrily sought-for bliss and dejection, those extreme offerings of sleepless nights spent at the writing table, and above all marriage and children. The identical source of these two restlessly meandering streams was most clearly revealed in his letters to Felice Bauer. This agonizingly protracted debate with himself and the poor victim of what sometimes he believed was his love, springs from the center—a center that most certainly could not hold—of Kafka's existence. That this was so would be shown if by nothing else by the very great (as may seem to some readers disproportionate) importance he attached to "her" story, "The Judgment," and even more by his ceaseless brooding on the meaning of her role in it. To concentrate on these letters at some length means to move within the light, and often within the impenetrable shadow, cast by the central mystery. It maintained its destructive position there almost to the very end and certainly throughout his affair with a woman very different from Felice, and this despite her energy, determined sexuality, and literary intelligence: Milena. It was only in the vicinity of death, during the last year of his life, that the mystery relaxed its grip of unhappiness and allowed for the grace of Kafka's one happy love relationship: with Dora Dymant (or Diamant), the Jewish-Chassidic girl from Eastern Europe, mistress of his months in Berlin, and nurse of his dying in the sanatorium in Kierling, near Vienna.

In one of his last letters to Felice (October 1, 1917), Kafka speaks of two beings that fight each other within himself; or rather he says that he *is* their fight and will perish in their struggle. Although in counting the number of pugnacious souls in his breast he makes, as it were, a mistake in his favor (for that fight is between many warriors, and every one of them fights every other), it is, so far as his writing is concerned, always a *duel* that is being fought out, with the duelists assuming the notorious German roles of Faust and Mephistopheles, even if they speak with the more fatigued voices of a later epoch. The one asks, after the manner of Goethe's Mephistopheles, whether there was anything worth reading in those works: *"Was ist daran zu lesen?"* Was the "eternal void" not preferable? *"Ich liebte mir dafür das Ewig-Leere."* Yet the other, despite his dejection, faintly hopes that thanks to his works at least a trace of his days on earth—*"die Spur von meinen Erdentagen"*—will be preserved throughout the eons; whereupon the first again tempts him with the question: What would be the use of that? Or, as the German-speaking Jews of Prague, Kafka's fellow citizens and guests of Café Arco, used to say: *"Und wenn schon!"* ("So what?") Kafka himself could not but resist the temptation of such indifference. Again and again he stared with a kind of passionate melancholy into the voids of the human spirit; and yet his craving for the spiritual consummation of the time given to him was equally impassioned. Therefore he was at no moment of his life and art capable of such skepticism. (Between "life" and "art" there senselessly officiates an "and" which, compelled by the rules of language, conjoins what are, for Kafka, one and the same and are yet—the demonic ambivalence—in irreconcilable opposition.) Kafka saw himself faced, ever anew, with incompatible possibilities: the fame of the artist, for instance, or the saving grace of oblivion (that oblivion which the last sentence of "Josephine" equates with a superior kind of redemption); marriage or the ascetic life. He wavered with such vehemence and intensity that from a distance his oscillations look like firmness. In such paradoxes lie the roots of Kafka's extraordinary genius, a genius that prompted Max Brod, its first discoverer, not to act in accordance with the text of his "will."

Hamlet, before him, suffered the same calamity. Hamlet's self-condemnations came from the same origin as Kafka's: from the discovery that his soul is subject to laws radically different from those that rule the incomprehensible "givenness" of the external life. How could Fortinbras, Kafka asks in his diary of September 1915, say that Hamlet had conducted himself truly like a king? Royal conduct where authentic existence has become impossible? For the authenticity of life rests upon the correspondence between the inner soul and the nature of the external world. Where this is lacking, authenticity becomes a chimera, and wavering is the only genuine action. It is the ethically most delicate persons who tend to blame themselves for this imbalance between mind and circumstance, this estrangement of the soul from the world (which for Hegel signaled the arrival of a whole predestined phase in history), and indict themselves for using actors' tricks, indeed, deceit, when in truth every outward sign or gesture—be it the rejection of the parental home, or the abandonment of a senseless profession, or marrying, or even the writing of words—is bound to strike them as a coarsely false designation of the inner state. On January 16, 1922, Kafka entered in his diary: "The clocks are not in unison; the inner one runs crazily on at a devilish or demonic or in any case inhuman pace, the outer one limps along at its usual speed. What else can happen but that the two worlds split apart, and they do split apart, or at least clash in a fearful manner." And before he wrote to Felice on October 1, 1917, describing his disease as only "outwardly" tuberculosis but, within, a weapon wielded by himself against himself (this, he said, is the reason why there could be no cure for him), she must have asked him whether he had always been truthful toward her. With the moral hypochondria of a man ready to *feel* guiltily responsible for what he *knows* to be a flaw in the order of the world, he answered that he had lied very little, given that his life could not be lived at all without *some* lies: "I am a mendacious creature; for me it is the only way to maintain an even keel, my boat is fragile." The balance that is impossible to keep without lying is surely that between the inner and the outer conditions; and the boat is unstable because it has been made according to a design that condemns it to shipwreck in an element in which it has been forced to move by a dispensation as mysterious as it seems malicious. But this confession, false in its outward simplicity, is followed by a typically Kafkaesque complication that comes closer to the truth. Yes, Kafka writes, he does want to deceive, "but without actual deception."

Just as Hamlet's "acting" is nothing but the theatrically effective code for a situation that compels the inner man to be someone else as soon as he becomes active in the external sphere, so Kafka's "deceiving without deception" is merely the honest but futile toll paid by language at the broken bridge over the gulf fixed between within and without. "Deceiving without deception": it is a milder version of the phrase with which Kafka characterized himself when in his diary he described the scene at the dissolution of his first engagement (July 23, 1914), "Devilish in my innocence." (The father in "The Judgment" accuses his son: "An innocent child, yes, that you were truly, but still more truly have you been a devilish human being.")

This is the question which Kafka's love letters—so different in this from any other love letters in literature —ask with terrible urgency: what was the nature of the relationship between Kafka and the things which, according to a universal convention he accepted with self-tormenting and quasi-religious determination, make up the world's external reality? Was his inner life related to the outer world in a "natural" manner? That is, in a manner expressible, if at all, not alone through his art—and even through his art only obscurely, for his is an art more poignantly and disturbingly obscure than literature has ever known. Even Milena, the love of a few years later, more intellectual and articulate than Felice, also more passionate and more successful in evoking his passion, and above all not expecting or waiting to be married to him, must have been, to judge by the letters he wrote to her, only too familiar with these questions—and the negative answers. She knew that the "essence of his being" was *Angst*, that anxiety which rises like a poisonous exhalation from the gap between a self and a world.

Suppose that Felice, long after these two futile wedding preparations in two cities, long after the termination of the engagement, perhaps long after Kafka's death, had gathered the courage to read his letters again and asked herself: was it really "I" whom he thought he loved? Would she not have discovered that "she" did not have any real existence on these sheets of paper? As the end of their liaison approached, Kafka said (in his diary of September 21, 1917) that the "real" Felice bore an excessive burden of "real" unhappiness, while he, artist and conjurer of the unreal, said of himself—perhaps unconsciously following the model of Goethe's Tasso (*"Und wenn der Mensch in seiner Qual verstummt, / Gab mir ein Gott, zu sagen, wie ich leide"*)—that where others would be silenced by their pain, he, in his suffering, with his "head still smarting from unhappiness," was yet able "to go beyond that and with as many flourishes as I have the talent for . . . ring simple, or contrapuntal, or a whole orchestra of changes on my theme" (September 19, 1917). Must she not have felt most terribly betrayed, although he had never deceived her intentionally, even if she recognized that nothing raised her so high as did the incandescent language of his letters? Yet from a cer-

tain moment on he plagued her continually with endless "changes" or variations on his own, deceptively
"selfless" versions of a sentence by Kierkegaard: "Marry
me, and you will regret it; marry me not, and you will
regret it; marry me or marry me not, and you will regret
either." "Was ever woman in this humour woo'd?"
Shakespeare put these words into the mouth of a great
villain. It is astonishing that they could also be used of
the peculiar saint who was Felice's fiancé.

2

Deeply problematical though Kafka's love was, it was
not more so than his attitude toward his writing; and
this is why the true executor of his "will"—the will that
decreed the destruction of his manuscripts—would have
had to be a magician, the producer of a sequence of
mythical scenes where Kafka's works, after being
burned, would rise again from the ashes, purified, in unheard-of beauty and perfection, consisting of nothing
but "sheer light, sheer freedom, sheer power, no shadow,
no barrier." Another absolutist in the history of German
literature once described in this way his highest poetic
aspiration; to attain to it, Schiller said, he would gladly
spend all the spiritual strength of his nature even if the
effort "were to consume me entirely." And Kafka, after
completing his story "A Country Doctor" in September
1917, confided to his diary that writing such stories
could still give him "passing satisfaction," but happiness he would know only if he succeeded in "raising the
world into the pure, the true, and the immutable." Often
it seems that Kafka had no will except this, and with
this will he aspired to a world which, according to
Schopenhauer, is the negation of the "world-as-will,"
a world in which no "last wills" have to be made, be-

cause it is purely spiritual;[1] and the never-satisfied claim
he made upon his art was that it should cleanse the
only true world, the spiritual one, of anything that was
not of the spirit by means of the absolute perfection
of language. Certainly, language is the most common
possession of all men: all people speak, just as in the
nation of mice everyone whistles, but only in the whis-
tling of Kafka's artist, the singing mouse Josephine, is it
"free from the fetters of daily life and it sets us free too
for a little while." Flaubert meant so much to Kafka
that he could have said of him what he once wrote to
Felice of Strindberg (October 26, 1916): "One has only
to close one's eyes, and one's own blood delivers lectures" about him. And it was Flaubert who once dreamed
of "writing a book about nothing at all, a book that
would have not the slightest bearing upon the external
world and would be held together entirely by the inner
force of its style."[2] This ambition, which in the case of
Flaubert appeared to aim at absolute aestheticism, with
Kafka took off the aesthetic mask and clearly showed
its religious features. Whenever he tried to convince
Felice that he must not marry, he almost always spoke
of his literary vocation as if its fulfillment depended
upon his keeping a monk's vow of celibacy. His Fifth
Octavo Note-Book contains this entry: "The world—F.
is its representative—and my ego are tearing my body
apart in a conflict that there is no resolving." And when
he thought he might resolve it after all, as, according
to the diary, he did on August 14, 1913, this was the
result: "Coitus as punishment for the happiness of being
together. Live as ascetically as possible, more ascetically

[1] On this decisive—and, with Kafka, decisively contradictory
—belief, see below, Chapter iii, on *The Trial*.
[2] Gustave Flaubert, *Oeuvres complètes—Correspondance*
(Paris, 1926–54), II, 345.

than a bachelor, that is the only possible way for me to endure marriage. But she?"

Only if his writing goes well has he the strength to live: he tells her this again and again, and as early as November 1, 1912, he confesses that, had he met her "during a barren period," he would never have been courageous enough to approach her. But if there is, for once, such rare abundance of productive energy, he must not waste it upon "living." For when he is deserted by his art, he feels forsaken by God and cannot live up to the demands of any human relationship. It is a truly vicious circle. Even in the initial stages of their correspondence she, with the instinct of a woman threatened by a powerful rival, obviously counseled him to be more moderate in his literary dedication. No, he replies in the same letter, he would be a "hopeless fool" if he did what she requests: "If I spare myself in this respect, I am not really sparing myself, I am committing suicide"; it is quite possible that his writing is "worthless," but if so, then he too is "definitely and without doubt worthless." And although his anxieties at the prospect of marriage seem sometimes prompted by the fear of sexual impotence, they are probably due much more to his misgivings about a manner of living that might be the betrayal of his inmost truth. Was not human sexuality more than anything else cursed with that curse which had upset the congruity between within and without? Was it not unavoidable that for him the unequivocal directness of the act of love should persistently be brought into question by inner voices denying that it was true to the complex inner state? One of these voices makes itself heard in a diary note of July 5, 1916: "The hardships of living together. Forced upon us by strangeness, pity, lust, cowardice, vanity, and only deep down, perhaps, a thin little stream worthy of the name of love, impossible to seek out, flashing once in the moment of a moment."

This he wrote during the few weeks that he spent in Marienbad with Felice, who then, most likely for the first time, was his mistress. Years afterward, those days shine in his memory with the light of a perplexed happiness, and yet even then they are recalled not without doubt and a little terror. At the end of January 1922 he was in the Bohemian resort of Spindlermühle. What would it be like, he asks in his diary, if Milena—the woman whose love dominated his life then—joined him there? Of course it would give him some pleasure, and yet it would be terrible: "I should be plunged into a world in which I could not live." And then, "It only remains to solve the riddle of why I had fourteen days of happiness in Marienbad." Whatever may be the solution of this riddle, one answer—according to his Marienbad diary entries—is that he was not all that happy, or at least, that his happiness did not last two weeks. In any case, whatever he may have felt six years before, he says in 1922 that it is too late. Let others be in love and make love; for himself, this is now unthinkable. "I am too far away, am banished." True, he has a few representatives in those regions "down there," but his main sustenance grows "from other roots in other climes."

Was it his writing that came from those roots or breathed that air? Sometimes he seemed to believe this. During such periods his "true life" consisted in defending his writing table, and happiness was in writing well. Melancholy threatened when he wrote badly, disaster when he reached a dead point. Then his laments sounded as if they were for a lost love; but he was referring to his stories when he spoke of their "withdrawing" from him, "rejecting" him, or "denying themselves"

to him. If for some time he was unable to write, he was
"in a void." On June 26, 1913, he wrote to Felice that
only in the depth of writing resided his center of gravity,
and he apparently had no notion how much she must
have been hurt by his telling her at the same time that
she had this much in common with his job (and she
knew of course that he detested it), that she too was
"on the surface of life." Thus a marriage with her would
be compatible with his office work but not with his
existence as a writer: for this he needed seclusion; no,
not—as she, perhaps quoting a favorite Chinese poem
of his, seems to have said—the seclusion of a hermit,
but that of a dead man. "Writing, in this sense, is a sleep
deeper than that of death, and just as one would not
and cannot tear the dead from their graves, so I must
not and cannot be torn from my desk at night." Indeed,
as early as the long letter he wrote to her during the
last night of "their" year 1912, the year of their first
meeting, he frightened her with the unintended cruelty
of his love constantly vacillating between literature and
marriage, this life and that life, this death and that
death. Taking up her naïve phrase "We belong together
unconditionally," he developed it as follows: "This, dearest, is true a thousandfold; now, for instance, in these
first hours of the New Year I could have no greater and
no crazier wish than that we should be bound together
inseparably by the wrists of your left and my right
hand." Why does this image occur to him? Perhaps, he
says, because a book about the French Revolution happens to lie before him, and because it is, after all, possible "that a couple thus bound together was once led to
the scaffold." But at this point he realizes what a weird
New Year's love letter this has become, and he exclaims,
"But what is all this that's racing through my head!"—
the same head that today had yielded hardly anything

useful for the continuation of the novel (*Amerika*): "That's the 13 in the new year's date." —This is what could happen when his thoughts turned to life and love.

3

Was Kafka's "true" life rooted in literature? It would of course be unduly simple to put it like this. An amateur graphologist whom Felice had met during a vacation "analyzed" Kafka's character for her from his handwriting, and she sent him the result. "The man in your *pension* should leave graphology alone," Kafka replied on August 14, 1913. For his findings are all wrong: neither is he, Kafka, "very determined" in his actions nor "extremely sensual"; on the contrary, he has a "magnificent, inborn capacity for asceticism." Nothing whatever in the dilettante's findings is correct, but the most absurdly false thing to say is that Kafka is interested in literature. There is no grain of truth in this, Kafka protests: "I have no literary interest, but am made of literature, I am nothing else and cannot be anything else." And then he goes on to tell her a little episode from a history of satanism he was just reading: A monk had the gift to sing so beautifully that everybody who heard him listened with sheer delight. But one day another cleric believed he recognized the voice of Satan in that loveliness and proceeded to exorcise him; and the singer, whose life resided entirely in his gift of song, dropped dead and his body began at once to decay.

"The relationship," Kafka comments, "between me and literature is similar . . . except that my literature is not as sweet as that monk's voice."[3] This means, as he warns

[3] To Milena he wrote seven years later: "No people sing with such pure voices as those who live in deepest Hell; what we take for the songs of angels is their song."

Felice again on August 22, 1913, that as his wife she would have to lead "a monastic life at the side of a man who is peevish, miserable, silent, discontented, and sickly," who "is chained to invisible literature by invisible chains." And two days later he affirms once more that he does not feel "attracted to writing," as she must have called it in a letter to him; no, certainly not, he answers, this is no attraction: an attraction "can be uprooted and crushed. But this is what I am." —It follows that what he expected of the executor of his "will" was aid in a kind of posthumous suicide.

He is nothing but literature, Kafka says so often, with such determination, and in such excellent prose as it could never be said by one who did not believe what he wrote. Yet not less frequently, and with equal determination, and surely not in worse prose, he says that for this reason he has forfeited his chances of salvation. No doubt it seemed to Kafka that his "true life" consisted in writing, that his whole existence had its "center of gravity" in the depth of literary creation, that through art alone he might raise the world into "the pure, the true, and the immutable," and that marriage or profession, indeed the whole world as perceived through the senses, was nothing but the evil in the only "real"—the spiritual—world, a world which art, and only art, could make accessible to the senses without itself falling a prey to evil. But it merely seemed so. "In reality" it was precisely at this point that the devil lay in wait for his chosen victim: for him who deluded himself with such superstitions. Kafka's faith in the high spiritual rank of his art was an intermittent one; more often he believed that art was his curse.

In the long letter that Kafka wrote to Max Brod on July 5, 1922, the condemnation of his art—and, it would seem, not only of his—reaches its climax. This negative judgment of art in its relationship to "life" naturally has a history, mostly written by artists themselves. Its stages in German literature are marked by Goethe's *Torquato Tasso* and *Pandora*, by the figure of Euphorion in *Faust II*, by Grillparzer's *Sappho* and his *Armer Spielmann* (a story very dear to Kafka), and by Thomas Mann's *Tonio Kröger*, *Death in Venice*, and, of course, *Doctor Faustus*. "Writing sustains me," Kafka wrote in that letter, as he used to say so often to Felice. But what sort of life is it that is thus sustained? An extremely questionable one: "Writing is a delicious reward. For what? During the last night the answer was as clear to me as a lesson meant for little children: reward for services rendered to the devil." And this is followed by Kafka's description, as grand as it is precise, of what he sees as devilish in writing: "This descent to dark powers, this unbinding of spiritual forces whose nature it is to be bound together, these dubious embraces and what else may go on down there that is forgotten when one writes one's stories in the light of the sun. Perhaps there is also another kind of writing. I know only this." Had Nietzsche lived to read this, the great "re-assessor of values" might have learned how easy it is to translate the "Dionysian"—for this is what Kafka here evokes—into the moral language of Judeo-Christianity, how quickly the intoxicated God can be transformed into the sober Satan. But who is the "one" that writes his stories in "the light of the sun"? Kafka himself? "The Judgment"—and sunlight? "The Metamorphosis," an "exceedingly nauseating tale," as he once described it to Felice (November 24, 1912)—and sunlight? *The Trial, The Castle*—and sunlight? What must it have been like "down below," if above such harvest ripened?

In his letters to Felice, Kafka never tired of indicting,

with apparently inexhaustible resourcefulness, the pursuit of literature as a form of living; and yet, although he delivered such accusations with a new passion and with heightened nervous sensibility, they had been in substance familiar for a very long time. Denunciations of the aesthetic mode of life had been uttered by Keats, certainly by Kleist, Grillparzer, Flaubert, Baudelaire, Rilke, again and again by Thomas Mann, and, with the support of a religious-existential philosophy, by Kierkegaard. For Kafka—as for Kierkegaard—this manner of existence is devilish because of the insatiable appetite for aesthetic enterprise with which the artist builds imaginary houses and palaces in order to look at them admiringly and offer them to the admiring inspection of other men, while as a "human being" he is without a home. "It is," Kafka wrote to Brod, the "unreality" of poetic existence that, more "mortal" than any other mortal life, "cannot last," is "not even made of dust," but is "a mere construction of the chase after pleasure." What others know as the self is, in the case of the poet, debarred from eternal life because it has lived not even once: "I have remained clay," Kafka wrote, "I have not used the spark for making fire but merely for illuminating my deadness." At the beginning of August 1914 —perhaps because Europe behaved at that time as if she insisted upon becoming more "real" every day—he noted in his diary with the utmost clarity the consumptive manner of his experiencing the real: "My talent for portraying my dreamlike inner life has thrust all other matters into the background." By "other matters" he meant World War I.

He demanded of Felice that she should write to him more and more often in order to assure him of his own self and their love in the only form truly appropriate to him (if he was not in the mood to implore her to write less, because the arrival of a letter made him incapable of dealing with the business of the day). Once, when she had obviously apologized for not having written a letter he expected, he replied (during the night of February 21–22, 1913): "Neither in the office nor in the tram could you write to me. Shall I tell you why, dearest? You didn't know whom to write to. I am no target for letters." For he does not really exist; he only exists, he believes, in the "unreality" of literature. And as soon as Grete Bloch, Felice's friend, dramatically enters this relationship (an entry that might have been fatal had her intervention been less episodic and the engagement not been fated in any case), the epistolary Eros, the god that mischievously prefers literary fantasies to real encounters of real persons, is on the verge of setting his amorous imagination on fire once again, as Kafka's letters betray. His imagination and his letter writing; for despite her playing an important if somewhat puzzling role at the little Berlin gathering where Kafka's and Felice's first engagement was terminated (Kafka, in subsequent letters, refers to Grete Bloch as "the judge"), it is most improbable that there ever was a "real" love affair between the two. In any case, she was still Felice's friend when Felice's engagement to Kafka was renewed in July 1917.[1]

Because he is a writer, he has lost the world; yet the world that he has gained in return (and a world it *is*: how else but in obedience to the norms of a real world could Kafka's language have acquired such classical lucidity?), the world of his "dreamlike inner life," strikes him again and again as an infernal delusion. Is not the

[1] My reasons for not giving credence to Grete Bloch's assertion, in 1940, that she was the mother of a child by Kafka are given in *Letters to Felice*, pp. 323f.

language of which his world is built, he asks, utterly deceptive in its clarity? What *is* the reality that it expresses? Perhaps it is not even correct to say that it corresponds to his own inner state. True, at times language appears to him as a refuge of his inwardness, deprived as this is of any external existence that would be appropriate to it. Then the power to write seems almost a salvation, "a merciful surplus of strength at a moment when suffering has raked me to the bottom of my being and plainly exhausted all my strength." Alas, this comes from the same section of his diary (September 1917) in which he also exhorts himself laconically: "Tear everything up." Again and again his words seem to him illusory, indeed fraudulent. "When I was in the swing of writing and living," he reminded Felice in a letter of March 17–18, 1913, "I once wrote to you that no true feeling need search for the corresponding words, but is confronted or even impelled by them." Yes, this is what he wrote "once," four weeks before, during the night of February 18–19, 1913, when he maintained that he would never lack the power to express perfectly what he wished to say, although false phrases might occasionally ambush his pen, get entangled in its nib, and be dragged into his letters. Yet all talk of the "weakness of language, and comparisons between the limitations of words and the infinity of feelings, are utterly wrong. The infinite feeling continues to be as infinite in words as it was in the heart. What is clear within is bound to become so in words as well." This he wrote in the vain and hopeful belief that there was at last *one* external sign that corresponded to the inner truth: good writing. Writing, therefore, afforded what every other activity in life denied: the authenticity of the outward gesture. But now not even this was true; now it was as if hardly a word reached him from its source; every single one was "seized upon fortuitously and with great difficulty somewhere along the way."

This is the curse: he is nothing when he cannot write; and he is in a different kind of nothingness if, rarely enough, he is, as he put it, "received" by his writing. As early as the first months of his correspondence with Felice (November 1, 1912), he tells her that whenever he is unsuccessful in his attempts to write, he lies collapsed on the floor, "fit for the dustbin." (He is clearly alluding to "The Metamorphosis," the "exceptionally repulsive story" in the making, where the charwoman applies the broom to the insect corpse of Gregor Samsa, and afterward laughingly announces to his parents and sister that they need not worry any more about "how to get rid of the thing next door.") And on November 29–30, 1912, Kafka, writing during a night that has been sleepless with frustration, promises Felice that in future he will behave more like an affectionate friend, for "surely I can't be utterly thrown out of my writing having thought more than once that I was sitting in its center, settled in its comforting warmth." Small wonder, then, that not so long after this sorrowful love letter (addressed, it would seem, more to his art than to Felice), during the night of January 14–15, 1913, when apparently his work is going well, he confides what surely must remain incomprehensible to her after his affectionate November promise: that, on the contrary, he will be a faithless husband because night after night he will commit adultery with his writing. Innocently, she had obviously told him that she would sit up with him while he was writing. No, he replies, that would make writing quite impossible for him because even the loneliest night was not night enough to give him the stillness and solitude he needs. Writing demands surrender without the slightest restraint, a degree of sincerity and honesty from which a man, "as long as he is in his right mind," must refrain in his dealings with other people, be it the most beloved person. For the ground on which he stands—or even on which two human beings stand together—begins to shake as soon as that "truer emotion" wells up in him which alone can give valid form to the work. "I have often thought that the best mode of life for me would be to sit in the innermost room of a spacious locked cellar with my writing things and a lamp. . . . And how I would write! From what depths I would drag it up! Without effort! For extreme concentration knows no effort. The trouble is that I might not be able to keep it up for long, and at the first failure—which perhaps even in these circumstances could not be avoided—would be bound to end in a grandiose fit of madness."

Only when Kafka lives entirely as a writer does he dwell in his truth. This truth is to be found nowhere else. For it is such that he who has lived with it must become insane if he is deprived of it; and life itself, the would in which marriages are made, for instance, *is* this deprivation. Would she please tell her "cellar-dweller" what she will think of that after she has become his beloved and deceived wife? Not much, would undoubtedly be her answer. But he saves her the trouble of it. Half a year later, in a letter of August 22, 1913, he remarks that if the truth of what he writes is to be measured in terms of the "real," the assessment would show an unfathomable disproportion, a disproportion to which much later, in a letter to Max Brod (July 20, 1922), he gives a simple and exact name: lie. At that time he had just read the memoirs of the German writer and poet Theodor Storm, and quoted to Felice the conversation Storm and the poet Eduard Mörike once had about Heinrich Heine, whom they both admired. Mörike said in his homely Swabian dialect: "He is a poet through and through, but not for a quarter of an hour could I live with him: because of the lie right in the middle of his being." Kafka commented: "And this is, at least seen from one angle, a brilliant summing up of what I think of the writer"—of *any* writer.

Once again, literature, which only a little while before had been the purest servant of truth, shaking to their foundations all illusory "realities," is itself the purest lie. And why? Because it demands of him who practices it, he who *is* literature, the abandonment of the real world. Is it then the real world that, after all, is in possession of the truth? There can be no doubt that literature and "reality" struck Kafka with ever renewed and tormenting force as incompatible; yet with his mind rapidly moving to and fro within the alternative, it remained uncertain in which realm truth was to be found. Is truth embedded in the written words (although, more often than not, these behave like the weak legs of his Hunger Artist, scraping "the ground . . . as if it were not really solid ground, as if they were only trying to find solid ground")? Or is truth in that world which the writer lost while he was making words?

Kafka's letters to Felice are the best commentary on his story "A Hunger Artist," since they endlessly debate the very theme that later assumed parabolic form in the story: the disproportion between the inner hunger and the nourishment offered by the external world, a disproportion that is both the main theme of the letters and the reason why the Hunger Artist must "fast, I can't help it." For had he ever found the food he liked, he would "have made no fuss" and eaten his fill, "like you or anyone else." At the same time, however, "A Hunger Artist" is also Kafka's incredibly acrobatic act of simultaneously affirming *and* denying the existence of both the Hunger Artist and the young panther which, after the artist's death from starvation, occupies his cage and whose exquisite animal body, equipped "almost to bursting point" with the necessities of life, is a pleasure for the gazing crowds to behold, although it is not easy for them to bear the hot breath of passion for life that streams from its throat. Apparently the passion for life has a bad smell.

The incompatibilities which merge and are artistically reconciled in "A Hunger Artist" are identical with those which make Kafka's letters to Felice an incomprehensible love story. Just as Rilke, in the seventh of the *Duino Elegies*, with one and the same gesture invokes and wards off the Angel, Kafka seeks to achieve marriage, an existence "within life," but not more zealously than he aspires to the ascetic solitude of the hermit in the cellar. In the letter of March 17–18, 1913, in which he speaks of the refusal of language faithfully to report the inner state, he also exclaims despairingly: "How could my writing to you, however firm my hand, achieve everything I want to achieve: To convince you that my two requests are equally serious: 'Go on loving me,' and 'Hate me!'" Two months later, during the night of May 12–13, he confesses that on the previous day, while getting ready to return to Prague from his Whitsun visit in Berlin, he had only one text in his head: "I cannot live without her, nor with her," and with these words, "I threw one thing after another into the bag, and felt something was about to explode in my breast."

4

It is not surprising that, torn by the tensions between within and without, and full of misgivings about himself, Kafka was tempted to side with the world. And how well the world sometimes fared in his care! Immeasurably better than it deserved! The writer who like no other anticipated in his imagination the horrors of an epoch that began with World War I, accepted the war itself in the matter-of-fact manner of the many who easily become reconciled to whatever happens. Moreover, Kafka eventually saw the war as his chance to escape into a real battle from the agony of the "unreal" one that went on in his brain and heart. On August 27, 1916, he noted in his diary: "There is no question of your first task: to become a soldier." He made several efforts in this direction, probably in the way he had made many other efforts: in the sure expectation of failure. Before the war, he never questioned the crisis-ridden and fragile reality of the late Hapsburg monarchy. In this respect he was, despite his episodic interest in an anarcho-socialist group in Prague, not different from any other loyal subject of the Emperor. Indeed, he was in the apocalyptic mood "to advocate retreat . . . for everything," as he said to Felice (October 27, 1912), because on the Balkan peninsula the political situation became more and more catastrophic for Austria. True, he detested the noisy processions of patriotic crowds hailing the Austrian declaration of war: these, he wrote in his diary, belonged to the most repugnant occurrences accompanying the war; and he turned even anti-Semitic by holding the Jewish merchants responsible for them, the people "who are German one day, Czech the next." Yet he blamed himself and not the event for whatever was negative in his feelings about the war. He was, he said, an "empty vessel" that was yet "full of lies, hate, and envy"; he discovered nothing but wickedness in his heart: "pettiness, indecision, envy, and hatred of those who are fighting." Later, on April 5, 1915, when Felice had obviously asked him whether the war made him suffer, he answered that, if he suffered, then it was mostly because "I myself am taking no part." One month later, on May 6, 1915, he wrote that he would be happy to become a soldier. Very soon he was to have his medical examination, and Felice should wish, as much as he did himself, that they would accept him.

If one seriously believes that Kafka is important for one's understanding of the age in which he lived and wrote, then, for a while at least, one ought to turn a deaf ear to the din of analyses that locate the causes of our wars and other troubles exclusively in colonialism, class struggles, and the dialectics of history. One ought to listen instead to the still voice with which a man, despairing of himself, opts for a world that cannot but destroy itself, spiritually forsaken as it is. In September 1912 Kafka wrote his first letter to Felice, whom, whether he knew it or not, he had sought out as his refuge from the onrush of his "ureality." Three months later, on New Year's Eve, he already had a distinct premonition of the final futility of his attempt to escape, and wrote her the astonishing letter which is, from beginning to end, true literature. In this letter he demanded her answer to a question. The ostensible form of the question is: would she put up with his fits of "unreality" or would she run away? He has put his question in "more than plain terms," he says, because he wants her answer to be overprecise and "independent from every point of view, even from that of reality" (overprecise to the point of the unreal—what an admirable characterization of his own work!). And he concludes with the wish to draw her "closer, closer, closer" to himself. At this point he appears to be overcome by the suspicion that he desires the impossible, since they live in different worlds, he in his own nonworld, and she—well, she in Berlin. "Where are you at this moment?" he asks, "from whose company am I drawing you away?" On the surface, to be sure, he meant only some New Year's Eve party, but as he roused himself from his letter, he may well have known how much he menacingly said: not "from whose company," but possibly from human society as such.

Overprecise to the point of the unreal: this is certainly true of the letter of October 27, 1912, in which, more than two months after the event, he describes to her the evening of August 13 when he met her for the first time. Testimony to love at first sight? To an eye immensely sharpened by that love? To a memory enhanced in its exactitude by the incipient passion? Possibly so: yet at the same time it is a document of that literary realism which has invited the epithet "magic," a document that, through hectic meticulousness, reveals the anxiety of an imagination which, more and more enclosed, fears that it might in the end forfeit the real altogether if it does not intensely watch over its every detail. In such hypnotically realistic description there is no trace to be found of that composure of mind with which, for instance, Homer describes the shield of Achilles, knowing that he can safely rely upon the solid reality of the shield as much as upon the appropriateness of his language to that reality. Instead of such equanimity, there is, with Kafka, the nervous desire to obtain from words a guarantee that "the real" has still some validity for the inner sense, that it still "counts." Baudelaire, in an essay on Théophile Gautier, said of Balzac's novels that they would be boring indeed if their author's inventories, so earnestly concerned with even the smallest matter, were not felt to be visionary; and indeed they are like Napoleonic wars through which the imagination hopes to recover and fortify a reality it is in danger of losing entirely.

An "empty face which wore its emptiness openly"— this is how Kafka's diary (August 20, 1912) describes Felice after their first meeting. Empty: thus it offers as much room as an empty page to the expansive imagination. And indeed, this imagination instantly falls in love, and before long word-storms, let loose in Prague, blow around the beloved empty face in Berlin. It begins on September 20, 1912, five weeks after their first and, for the time being, only meeting in the midst of other people, and starts with "My dear Fräulein Bauer." This letter, rather significantly, happens to coincide with the onrush of that sustained literary inspiration which, among other writings, produced "The Judgment." And "My dear Fräulein Bauer" rises, driven on by the imagination and the written word, to "Dear Fräulein Felice" and "Dearest Fräulein Felice," ultimately to the ecstatic *"Du"* of November 14, 1912, erupting in the letter that addresses her as "Dearest." Yet this embrace on the paper of the imagination is certainly no token of an early rendezvous. When Felice suggests a Christmas meeting in the "external reality" of Berlin, Kafka refuses, saying that he must use the few free days for his writing. And he does; but what he writes is mainly letters to her.

This is the onset of years filled with the agonies of struggle—not the struggle for this woman, whom he could have taken as his wife at any time he chose if he truly wanted a home in this world, but the struggle for the reality of world, marriage, and home. It is moving and at the same time terrifying to watch his words: how, in their entrancing dexterity they woo this "reality" of hers, those fragments of reality he gathers in through this correspondence, and how they maintain the precarious state of balance between the real and the literary. And all the time they are on the verge of becoming literature themselves, indulging in mythologizing, now abysmally sad and now again comical. In an instant Kafka can transform the real pain with which he awaits Felice's letters into the occasion for writing a comedy scene, in which his office staff, Mergl, Wottawa, and Böhm, appear as three comic *postillons d'amour*, trained to bring him with the utmost haste the letters arriving from Berlin. Or, having urged Felice time and again to describe her every day in minute particularity, he endows this or that triviality she reports with the quality of a mythic moment: the nocturnal signal, for instance, with which she announces to her mother that she has come home. Or he implores her to send him photographs, and more and more photographs, this paper currency of real moments devalued by every passing hour; and as soon as he holds them in his hands, he loses himself in the intense contemplation of those shadow appearances which, like the face in its outer emptiness, allow the inner gaze to descend into the depths of the imagination and at the same time maintain the illusion that its attention is fixed upon the reality of what is so realistically depicted; and he studies these mechanical reproductions as if they were all veiled images of a goddess who vaguely promises that one day she might reveal herself and with herself the mystery of the meaning of life. (The initial chapters of what is in many ways the Felice novel, *The Trial*, reflect most conspicuously this fascination with photographs.) When the correspondence turns to the reality, approaching menacingly, of the marriage quarters and the question of how to furnish them, the sumptuous stuff Felice purchases turns momentarily into a brood of dragons obstructing the knight's progress toward his beloved. Everything he does comes to the same: it perfectly succeeds as literature, and perfectly fails in coming to grips with the real situation.

Only once do Kafka's letters fill themselves with more reality: after the couple's stay in Marienbad during the summer of 1916. At that time, a Jewish People's Home was founded in Berlin. Felice helped there in looking after war refugees, particularly children, from Eastern Europe, and Kafka immersed himself in her pedagogical problems, encouraged and counseled her, recommended reading matter for her or her pupils, sent her parcels of books, and attended with sagacity and common sense to the real. The first contact with a real, even social and national, effort that struck him as good and sensible— and of course it came about through her activity, not his —calmed his mind for a while, although he told her in a letter of September 12, 1916, that on examination it would become clear that he was not a Zionist. This was probably due to his suspicion that the "normalization" of the Jews in a national state would endanger exactly that which he regarded as the most valuable Jewish quality, found above all among East European Jews: a particular kind of religiousness and spirituality, something that was "unreal," but unreal, for once, in a positive sense. Be that as it may, the time was very brief in which it seemed that he and Felice might found their life together upon something real. His anxieties returned, if anything more intensely than before. Despite this, there was the second engagement. Yet soon afterward Kafka suffered the hemorrhage, symptom of the disease from which, as he knew, he would never recover. It was, as he said in a letter of October 1, 1917, not "really" tuberculosis but the sign of his "general bankruptcy"; the blood did not come simply from the sick lung, but from the wound that one of the two enemies fighting within him had inflicted upon the other.

No doubt the enemies were real, for Kafka really died of this wound. It would nonetheless be rash to say that reality proved stronger in the end than literature—or that to which, following Kafka's usage, we have given the modest name of literature. Literature for him was not *just* literature. Despite the devilish suspicions he indefatigably uttered against it, it remained the only means by which he tried to give perfect form and shape to his life, a life which, after all, did not quite reject the demand for meaning, or at least allowed meaning to shine faintly from the depth through layers and layers of the meaningless that had all but covered it up. He wrote in order to secure this faint and elusive promise. Indeed, Kafka is not altogether wrong in saying to Felice that he is nothing but literature—real literature. Almost everything he wrote possesses an indisputable reality and "being" that are rare in modern writing and transcend most realities of the age. In this sense, too, his letters to Felice are, like himself, literature. Even after the "real" Felice receded from his life, her literary presence remained powerful. Kafka's diary (July 23, 1914) speaks of the strange family gathering in a Berlin hotel room, where on July 12, 1914, his engagement with her was revoked, as the *"Gerichtshof,"* the tribunal, the Court of Justice—and three weeks later he began writing *The Trial.* Although the presentation in it of the relationship between Joseph K. and F. B. is at least as heavily veiled as everything else in that fragmentary novel, it is yet clear enough that Kafka's diary interpretation of "The Judgment"—that Georg Bendemann perishes because of his fiancée—might also be applied to the mysterious design of guilt and punishment drawn around K. and the woman named with the initials of Felice Bauer.

The Trial

I

There is only one way to save oneself the trouble
of interpreting *The Trial*: not to read it. Not
reading it would be, moreover, the only available
manner of fulfilling Kafka's wish that all his un-
published writings should be destroyed. For to
take advantage of the contrary decision made by
Max Brod and to read the book is to become an
interpreter; and this in a much more radical
sense than applies to all intelligent reading.
Goethe, in the Preface to his *Theory of Colours*,
says about any experience of the mind: "Looking at a thing gradually issues in contemplation,
contemplation is thinking, thinking is establishing connections, and thus it is possible to say
that every attentive glance which we cast on the
world is an act of theorizing." For the same rea-

son one may say that every attentive glance at a text is an act of interpreting. But this, Goethe adds, ought to be done with the consciousness that it *is* an interpretation, and therefore, "to use a daring word, with *irony*"—a quality oppressively absent from the minds of many literary commentators who go through their texts with the professional air of policemen searching for the "meaning" as if it were contraband or stolen property. Their findings more often than not tend to provoke the question: If *this* is what the author meant, why did he not say so?

In the case of Kafka, and *The Trial* in particular, the compulsion to interpret is at its most compelling, and is as great as the compulsion to continue reading once one has begun: the urgencies are identical. For Kafka's style—simple, lucid, and "real" in the sense of never leaving any doubt concerning the reality of that which is narrated, described, or meditated—does yet narrate, describe, or meditate the shockingly unbelievable. While it is in the nature of Biblical parables to *show* meaning, through concrete images, to those who might be unable to comprehend meaning presented in the abstract, Kafka's parables seem to insinuate meaninglessness through nonetheless irrefutably real and therefore suggestively meaningful configurations. "The most wondrous poetic sentences are those which make us see, with indisputable certainty and great clarity, the physically impossible: they are true descriptions through words," Hugo von Hofmannsthal said with regard to Novalis.[1] It might carry even greater conviction if it were applied to Kafka, perhaps with the rider that in his case the "physically impossible" makes us see not the

---

[1] Hugo von Hofmannsthal, *Aufzeichnungen* (Frankfurt am Main, 1959), p. 138.

miraculous, as sometimes happens with Novalis, but infinite expanses of meaninglessness endowed with whatever meaning its "true description through words" is capable of yielding.

Yes, it is so! is what Kafka's reader is made to feel, only to look up and add, "It cannot be." It is the most sensible vision of an insensible world that produces this dizzying simultaneity of Impossible! and Of course! That Gregor Samsa of "The Metamorphosis" wakes up one morning to find himself transformed into a giant insect is reported without the slightest vestige of the fuss usually accompanying the fantastic. Does the narrated event, therefore, persuade us to suspend our disbelief? Not in the least; but as if we watched an unheard-of natural phenomenon, we are forced to ask: What does it mean? Again like an unheard-of natural phenomenon, it defies any established intellectual order and familiar form of understanding, and thus arouses the kind of intellectual anxiety that greedily and compulsively reaches out for interpretations.

"The right perception of any matter and a misunderstanding of the same matter do not wholly exclude each other." This is what the priest in *The Trial* affirms— talmudistically to the point of caricature—concerning the flawed understanding which the doorkeeper in the legend "Before the Law" has of his duty (which consists in keeping watch at the gate leading to the interior of the Law). Of the many divergent opinions which interpreters of the legend have entertained, the priest says: "The text is unalterable, and the interpretations are often merely expressions of the despair engendered by this." Did Kafka make him say this, prophetically, also of his own texts and their future interpreters? The legend "Before the Law" is at the heart of the novel and harbors its secret in the way Kafka's best stories harbor

their secrets: unyieldingly and only occasionally allowing for those glimpses of illumination that blind rather
than enlighten.

Joseph K., high official of a Bank, mysteriously tried
by a sordidly mysterious Court of Justice for a mysterious offense he is accused of having committed
against a mysterious law, has been waiting in the Cathedral for an Italian businessman to whom he was to
show the artistic monuments of the city. His waiting
has been in vain. (With Kafka *all* waiting is futile,
although it is also right to say of it what a character in
the novel says: that it is not the waiting that is useless
but only action; or, as the prophet Daniel pronounces:
"Blessed is he that waiteth.") The guided tour of the
Cathedral is not to take place. In any case, it would have
been impossible to see the works of art inside the Cathedral for the darkness of the winter morning is growing
ever darker and is finally impenetrable; the reader joins
K. in wondering whether winter clouds are its sufficient
cause. The blackness soon reveals its symbolic character
when the priest (who turns out to be the Court's prison
chaplain), angered by K.'s persistent defamatory remarks about the Court, shouts at him, "Can you not see
two steps ahead of you?"

"You are Joseph K.," says the priest from his pulpit,
and then warns him of the bad prospects of his trial.
"Yet I am not guilty," K. once again maintains. This
time he adds the question of whether guilt has any place
at all in human affairs: "We are all human beings here,
every one of us," implying: human beings with their
inevitable failings. "True," replies the cleric, "but this
is how the guilty tend to speak." When K. complains
about the bias of the Court and once again about its
corruption, the priest, descended from the pulpit, ad-
monishes him not to misjudge the character of the

Court—after the fashion of his misjudging the door-keeper in the legend "Before the Law" which he now narrates.

The legend, which according to the priest is part of the prefatory explanations introducing the Law itself, tells of a man from the country who arrives at the entrance gate of the Law. There he encounters the door-keeper. He asks to be admitted. The doorkeeper refuses: "Not now," he says. "Perhaps later?" asks the man. "It is possible," is the doorkeeper's reply, "but not now." There never will be "now." The man from the country is kept waiting forever. Having vainly entreated and even bribed the doorkeeper, and having become so familiar with him that he knows "even the fleas in his fur collar," he is, after years and years, about to die. He asks his final question:

> "Everyone strives to attain the Law . . . how does it come about, then, that in all these years no one has wanted to be admitted but me?" The door-keeper recognizes that the man is approaching his end and in order to reach his hearing that fails, he bellows in his ear: "No one but you could gain admittance through this door, since this door was meant for you alone. I am now going to shut it."

The parable "Before the Law" is the only part of *The Trial* that Kafka, with infallible discrimination, published himself. Despite its familiarity, it has retained its terrible charm and shows all the characteristic features of Kafka's art at its most powerful—possessing, that is, the kind of power that is in the gentle wafting of the wind rather than in the thunderous storm, and is the more destructive for it. Parodying Biblical simplicity, *sancta simplicitas*, it expresses the most unholy complications of the intelligence and raises hellish questions in the key of the innocently unquestionable. Its humor is at the same time tender and cruel, teasing the mind with the semblance of light into losing itself in the utmost obscurity.

It may have been from sheer benevolent consideration for the reader that Kafka did not let the parable, as its own aesthetic will seems to demand, stand by itself. In *The Trial*, he supplemented it with pages of exegesis that encroach upon its sovereignty but for once fore-stall any interpretative maneuvers: the writer himself demonstrates their futility. For instance: Has the door-keeper deceived the man from the country? Joseph K. feels immediately certain he has, but the priest exhorts him not to judge too rashly and above all not to venture outside the text; the text allows for no such condemna-tion of the doorkeeper; all that we come to know is that the man is not permitted to enter *now*, even though this particular entrance is meant only for him. It is not the doorkeeper's fault that the moment never comes which would redeem the supplicant as well as the very existence of the door. (Doors in Kafka's writings appear to be an architectural invention for the purpose of pre-venting people from entering.)

There is not the slightest hint to be found anywhere in the text that the doorkeeper—humble because he is only the lowest in the hierarchy of the Law, and yet powerful because he is, after all, in the Law's service—violates his commission by not admitting the man at that particular moment or at any particular time. It has to be assumed that he acts in accordance with the Law. Why should he act otherwise? From a capricious dis-like of the man? On the contrary, it may be from kind-ness that—at least in the opinion of many learned inter-preters—he goes beyond the call of duty by allowing the man to know that at some future time his request may be granted. Or is he corrupt in accepting gifts? The text does not support the conclusion that such acceptance is against the Law, although it would no doubt be against the Law if the doorkeeper let himself be seduced by bribes. Is there any reason for not believing him when, with the accent of Kafka's wit and the logic of the Hapsburg bureaucracy, he says that he only takes the man's presents to comfort the giver with the certainty that he has tried everything in his power? And so the exegetical dialogue between Joseph K. and the priest continues, leaving no pebble of interpretation unturned, and then throwing all of them away as worthless missiles, unfit to make so much as a dent in the armor of the mysterious futility. "The text is unalterable, and the interpretations are often merely expressions of the despair engendered by this."

Is there any fissure in it, undetected by Joseph K. and left unprotected by the priest? It seems there is not. We have heard the priest say that the correct comprehension of any matter *and* its misunderstanding are not entirely incompatible; and this paradox—like all good paradoxes, a splendid performance of the mind, induced by the castration of logic—was prompted by the observation that the doorkeeper was both right and wrong with regard to his office. In this respect he gives the impression of being simple-minded as well as conceited. True enough, his power is considerable, yet his manner suggests that he is unaware of the measure of his subordination. He conducts himself after the fashion of "great men" and does not seem to recognize that in some respects the man from the country might well be superior to him: he is free and has made the journey on his own volition, possessed as he is by the desire to come to know the Law. The doorkeeper, on the other hand, has long since accepted (if indeed it has not al-

ways been a matter of indifference to him) his lack of
courage in not daring to face even the third of the many
other doorkeepers on the way to the Law, not to mention the fact that he is bound by the Law to stay in the
place assigned to him, while the man from the country
is free to leave if he so wishes—like Joseph K. himself,
from whom, in the parting words of the priest, "the
Court wants nothing. . . . It receives you when you
come and it dismisses you when you go." The doorkeeper does not even know the Law that he so obediently
serves—just as the Whipper of the Court, in one of the
most disquieting episodes in this disquieting book,
cruelly and incorruptibly beats the "culprits" assigned
to him without questioning the assignment, and responds to Joseph K.'s attempt to ransom the victim by
saying: "I refuse to be bribed. I am commissioned to
whip, and whip I shall' (an anticipation of that evil
honesty and conscientiousness which later was to beget
the most abhorrent deeds in the regions of Kafka's
birthplace).

Compared even to the pitiable condition of the man
from the country, shrunk and blind and deaf in the end,
the doorkeeper is an obtuse creature. The story does not
record that, with his eyes intact, he has ever seen what
the man in his blindness perceives: the immense radiance streaming forth from the Law. Also, as some of
the fictitious commentators of the legend believe, he
may be deluded or be bragging or be cruelly determined
to inflict grief and regret upon the man in his last moments when he tells him that now, in the hour of the
man's death, he is going to shut the door that was meant
only for him. Has he the power to do so? Has it not
been said at the beginning of the parable that the entrance to the Law is always open? This "always" cannot
possibly be affected by the death of the individual.

Nevertheless, despite all his failings, the doorkeeper is, as the priest affirms, a servant of the Law and as such "beyond human judgment." Therefore it ought after all not be assumed that he is really inferior to the man from the country. To be enlisted by the Law, even as the lowest of doormen, is incomparably more than to live freely in the world; and to doubt this guardian's worthiness is to doubt the Law itself. Thus speaks the priest—not unlike K.'s lawyer, who advises him early in the novel that often it is better to be in chains than to be free. But at this point Joseph K. disagrees with the priest; if he were right, one would have to believe that everything the doorkeeper says is true; and has not the priest himself proved that this is impossible? No, the priest replies, one need not accept everything as true, "one must only accept it as necessary." K. calls this a "melancholy opinion": it holds that the order of the world is based upon a lie. This Joseph K. says "in conclusion," but Kafka sees to it that it is "not his final judgment." "The simple story had lost its clear outline, he wanted to put it out of his mind and the priest, who now showed great delicacy of feeling, suffered him to do so and accepted his comment in silence, although undoubtedly he did not agree with it."

Kafka's art of conclusively stating inconclusiveness is unsurpassed and probably insurpassable, and unbreachable seem the fortifications he builds to protect the mystery from the onslaughts of dogma, opinion, or conviction. Merely to protect the mystery from them? No, to deprive dogmas, opinions, and convictions of the air they need for breathing. And if they were as firm as rocks they would become like the sand of the desert, blown hither and thither by the wind and blinding even the most determined believer. Yet there is one certainty that is left untouched by the parable as well as by the whole book: the Law exists and Joseph K. must have most terribly offended it, for he is executed in the end with a double-edged—yes, double-edged—butcher's knife that is thrust into his heart and turned there twice. Three years before Kafka began to write *The Trial*, he had, on November 11, 1911, entered in his diary: "This morning, once again after a long time, I took pleasure in imagining that a knife was being turned in my heart," and as late as 1921 (October 20) he recorded a dream in which there was ". . . happiness . . . in the fact that I welcomed so freely, with such conviction and such joy, the punishment when it came."[2] But there is no joy in *this* punishment; it comes to Joseph K. in a deserted quarry on the periphery of the city, while the casements of a window on the top floor of a neighboring house fly open and a human figure stretches his hands out toward the scene of horror. The questions, evoked by this apparition and presumably issuing from Joseph K.'s mind, might be taken to point toward a miscarriage of justice: who was the person at the window? "A friend? A good man? . . . Someone who wanted to help? Was it one person only? Was it mankind?" The friendliest impulses of mankind, then, may well be working against the Court's administration of justice and may side with its unhappy victim. But, on the other

[2] The thought of dying in this manner must have obsessed Kafka's imagination. Even in his earliest story, "The Description of a Struggle," written about 1904, the following thought suddenly breaks the peace of the "I" 's nocturnal walk with an apparently harmless companion. ". . . this is the time for the murder. I'll stay with him and slowly he'll draw the dagger—the handle of which he is already holding in his pocket—along his coat, and then plunge it into me. It's unlikely that he'll be surprised at the simplicity of it all—yet maybe he will, who knows? I won't scream, I'll just stare at him as long as my eyes can stand it."

hand, the gestures of the figure up there might be mere projections of K.'s will to live, rising up in vain against the secret logic of the case, this logic being unshakable —and yet, we read—"it cannot withstand a man who wants to go on living."

Alas, it can, and Joseph K. dies "like a dog!" These are his last words; and if the reader's terrified revulsion leaves him capable of reflecting, he might find them somewhat inappropriate. For this is not how dogs are killed. Rather does it resemble the matador's way of killing the bull; and although no perfect metaphor is perfectly fitting, we come a little closer to it by remembering the episode with the painter Titorelli, the amiable charlatan and lover of children, confidant of Court officials and their only licensed portraitist, who adorns his portraits of the judges with the allegorical figure of Justice in a kind of personal union with the winged and dynamic goddess of victory. "Not a very good combination," says K. "Justice must stand still, or else the scales will waver, and a just verdict will become impossible." But still worse, after a few more strokes of Titorelli's crayon there emerges, dominating the previous image, the goddess of the hunt. But this is in blatant contradiction to what one of the warders, who come to arrest Joseph K., says of the Court: its officials "never go hunting for guilt in the populace but are drawn toward the guilty . . . and must send out us warders."

There is no end to such contradictions and ambiguities in *The Trial*. No end: the novel was doomed to remain a fragment and, as a novel, had to fail, even though Kafka did write the final chapter. As a conclusion to whatever might have been the whole work, it too is a failure, despite its superbly sustained, quietly sensational tone of narration, which is a little reminiscent of the last pages of Stendhal's *Le Rouge et le noir*. It fails in aesthetic and—which in this case is the same— ethical logic. For a nightmare will not become a novel even if it is pursued and elaborated through episode after episode. And an ending, unquestionable in its stark finality, is aesthetically and ethically offensive if it is supported only by a sequence of arbitrarily protractile scenes, all showing a presumed culprit who, not know- ing the nature of his guilt, helplessly casts about for help; or the sordidness and corruption of the judiciary order (at least in its lower echelon, and we come to know only this); or the clownish irresponsibility of those who claim to be able to assist the accused in his des- perate struggle for acquittal. What *is* his guilt? What *is* the Law?

It is the secret of Kafka's art almost to silence such questions. They are laughed out of court, as it were, by demons mischievously squatting in the empty spaces between the questions and the sought-for answers. Boorish curiosity in the company of tragic subtleties! And do such questions not miss the very point of *The Trial*? Yet, such is the mechanism of the moral and aesthetic sensibility that even the most accomplished description of a death sentence carried out with studied violence by two men looking like "tenth-rate old actors" —"What theatre are you playing at?" K. asks them— must affect us, in the absence of any answers to those questions, like the indiscretion of a sadistically bad dream told in public.

2

Even if it were possible to suppress those unsophisti- cated questions—what is the Law, what is the guilt?— for short spells of shock and intense captivation, it would be unfeasible in the long run, and it is the long run that accounts for the decisive flaw of *The Trial*. There is a certain tiresomeness in those ever-repeated descriptions of the Court's enormously complicated structure with its higher judges never visible or reachable; in the assertions, made again and again, of the infallibility of the Court's involvements so that there is always guilt where it becomes active ("Once it has brought a charge against someone, the Court can never be dislodged from that conviction," we learn from Titorelli, among others); in the reiterated characterizations of the accessible seats of justice and all its agencies as dirty, corrupt, oppressive, unaired, and fostering sexual exploitation.

All this, however, is as nothing compared to the structural imbalance which in the end threatens to bring down the building: the ever-present difficulty, that is, of reconciling the glorious presence and unquestioned validity of the invisible Law with the inglorious existence and dubious character of its mundane executants; or the radiance that pours forth from the interior of the truth (perceived, characteristically, only by the country man grown blind with age) with the fleas in the fur coats of its guardians; or the beauty which the Law appears to bestow upon those who are indicted in its name ("The accused are all beautiful," says the Lawyer, explaining why his maid Leni is so much attracted to K.) with the terrible fate it holds in store for them. Not that it would be hard to make one's peace with the contrast between the impurity of the creature and the pure light that is the essence of the Creator: Jews and Christians have learned this much in school. But in Kafka's novels, certainly in *The Trial*, original sin is as it were too sinful by half, and yet must—confusingly—be thought of as the richest source of virtue.

It is not easy to apply the story of the Fall to the case of Joseph K., although certainly it has some bearing. Kafka was convinced that he understood "the Fall of Man better than anyone"; but if he intended to make *The Trial* into an allegory of original sin, he certainly did not succeed and indeed was bound to fail, if for no other reason than because the *universality* of the Biblical disaster cannot be represented through the very particular destiny of one person, an ordinary person at that, or even of many persons, in contrast to the rest of mankind.[3] Or is the reader to believe that the Manufacturer or the Assistant Director of K.'s Bank—to name only two characters from the novel—is immune from the malady caused by the apple, although they may never have breakfasted on apples, as K. does on the morning of his arrest? His sin must be a particular one, even if it is rooted in the universal one; must be a sin not shared

---

[3] The nineteenth-century German dramatist Friedrich Hebbel tried to solve a similar problem by choosing as his hero or heroine a person equipped with quite extraordinary gifts, thus symbolically creating *the* individual because this *exceptional* individual is more of an individual than others: Agnes Bernauer through her surpassing beauty, Siegfried through his exceptional strength. But this is not what Kafka does with Joseph K. A passage in the "Letter to His Father" comes close, in personal and domestic terms, to stating, if not explaining, the relationship between Joseph K., the Law, and the rest of the world: "The world was for me divided into three parts: one in which I lived under laws which had been invented only for me and which I could, I did not know why, never completely comply with; then a second world, which was infinitely remote from mine, in which you lived, concerned with government, with the issuing of orders, and with the annoyance about their not being obeyed; and finally a third world where everybody else lived happily and free from orders and from having to obey." Although this is strikingly relevant to *The Trial*, it also shows the distance between a personal situation and its literary "mythological" transformation.

by the Manufacturer or Assistant Manager; and, to deserve the sentence of death, must be more substantial than the crumbs of guilt the moral reader may pick up in the course of the novel—K.'s loveless sexuality, his indifference to his mother, or his lack of courage in not interfering with the whipping of the boarders (in a scene, moreover, that is too dreamlike for moral judgments to rush in).

If there is any explanation for Kafka's ruinous compulsion to insist at the same time and in the same work upon the ultimately incompatible, the goodness of the Law and the evil of its application, it may be found in the pathology of his spiritual imagination, now quasi-Manichaean and now again drawn toward an emphatic and emphatically worldly yea-saying. "There is nothing but a spiritual world," he wrote in his "Reflections on Sin, Suffering, Hope, and the True Way," "and what we call the world of the senses, is the Evil in the spiritual world." Therefore any attempt to translate the spiritual into the tangibly concrete—and what else is the business of art or that of the worldly administering of Justice?—is with him in constant danger of yielding nothing but evil. Let the Law shine in transcendent brightness behind the last gate of reality; its secular execution is, with inexorable logic, entrusted to "the scoundrels of the Court's lower order," as Kafka puts it in the chapter "The Whipper." To turn to them in the expectation of justice is to hope for consolation from fleas; and as in the physical domain all individual life ends in death, so the stabbing in the quarry awaits him who is guilty of living in the world. For, as another Manichaean saying of Kafka's—in the same series of aphorisms—will have it: "The fact that there is nothing but a spiritual world deprives us of hope and gives us certainty." We need not ask what certainty. It is, in this "unreal" world, abrupt and deadly, even if the spirit is bound "hopelessly" to survive in the "only real" world.

Guilty of living? Of living in the world? If Kafka's imagination had simply been received into the Manichaean heresy, and if it had come to rest with the assurance that, as he put it in that sequence of "Reflections," "there can be knowledge of the diabolical but no belief in it, for there is nothing more diabolical than what exists," we would no longer have to ask why, in contrast to the luminosity of the invisible and unreachable Law, its doorkeepers are so dismal, its judges so mischievous, and its executioners so devilish. The unhappy but simple answer would be: because they exist. Kafka's terrible observation about knowledge, belief, and evil will have it that the whole world of the senses, the world "as we know it," is so perfect a realization of the diabolical as to leave no room for *believing* in evil; this is so because the proper object of *belief* is not the empirical but the transcendental world, the world not of the senses but of the spirit. The empirical world—and that, according to the aphorism, means Evil—is the province of *knowledge*. Thus it makes good sense for someone to say, "I believe in God," but it makes no sense (except, in English, a vaguely idiomatic one) to believe in doorknobs, influenza, or—the diabolical. If, therefore, it would be correct to assume that for Kafka the officials of the Court are, because they act in the world, *necessarily* corrupt, his would be a frightening but logically consistent world. Yet it is not. For Kafka means K.—and meant himself—to be guilty at the same time of an insufficiency in living *here and now*, of a lack of *faith in life*, the very life that is nonetheless seen as "the Evil in the spiritual world," indeed as the devil itself.

Never before has an artist so compulsively tried to hold simultaneously and weld together in works of art such irreconcilably contrary beliefs. Kafka, it seems, did exactly this in *The Trial*, and this is why the novel confronts the reader and interpreter not so much with difficulties as with inescapable defeat. For he who denied the reality of any world but that of the spirit, and who saw in life as it is lived the incarnation of the devil, *also* said that "in the struggle between yourself and the world you must take the side of the world"—"One must not cheat anyone, not even the world, of its victory"—and said it immediately before he reduced the world of the senses to nothing but "the Evil in the spiritual world." And entering the sphere in which *The Trial* is domiciled, we hear him say (a little later in the same collection of aphorisms) that we are "sinful not only because we have eaten of the Tree of Knowledge, but also because we have not yet eaten of the Tree of Life. The state in which we are is sinful, irrespective of guilt." We have lost Paradise by our sinfully being cast into the world, but then we have sinned once more, this time against the world, by not living in it courageously and abundantly. For Kafka's Tree of Life is certainly not the other tree in Eden that the Lord felt he had to protect from so ambitious a creature as man, intent upon himself becoming God, but is a tree that grows in the fields cultivated by Adam and Eve in the sweat of their brows.

"Marrying, founding a family, accepting all the children that come, supporting them in this insecure world and even guiding them a little is, I am convinced, the utmost a human being can succeed in doing at all," Kafka wrote in the "Letter to His Father," accusing his parent of having stood between him and this good life. Instead of leading this good life, he became, as we have heard him say, "literature": "I . . . am made of literature, I am nothing else and cannot be anything else."

Where is now the spiritual world with its claim to being the only true reality—*if* indeed Kafka ever found his spiritual reality in his art? Certainly, we know that at times he bitterly lamented the absence of any such reality from his living, that, as he said to Max Brod in the long letter of July 1922, he remained clay because he did not use the spark for lighting a fire but merely for illuminating his deadness, that is, for making literature.

Yet in another letter to Felice (March 17–18, 1913) he had equated being fully alive with having the inspiration to write. But then again he could not marry her— "everything in me revolted against it," he wrote in his diary (March 9, 1914)—because "marriage would have endangered my literary work." Elsewhere, in the letter to Brod, he again condemns literary work, not because it is bad but because it is evil. He is "sustained" by it, yet the life thus sustained is dedicated to serving "the devil." But at another time, among the fragments of *Wedding Preparations*, this mingling with the powers of darkness, his writing, appears to him as "a form of prayer"; and recording in his diary the commotion ensuing upon Austria's mobilization in the summer of 1914, he vows that he must at all costs continue writing, for this is *his* "struggle for self-preservation." The circle could not be more vicious. It is a paranoid situation that, were it not for his literary powers of resistance, would probably have developed into insanity.

Kafka knew this himself. To Brod he spoke of the terrible enslavement of the writer by his writing table: "He must never move away from it, must hold onto it with all his might, if he does not want to fall into madness." This, even today, is not likely to be true of many writers and would have been received as a crazy notion by most before the nineteenth century, for then, as Baudelaire put it with a grand and imprecise gesture, the poetic consciousness was an inexhaustible source of delights; afterward, he believed, it became "an inexhaustible arsenal of torture instruments."[4]

This reads as if anachronistically Baudelaire had had Kafka in mind; certainly the product of Kafka's servitude at the writing desk shows symptoms of the madness which the writing kept from breaking out in real life: the terrible logic of the absurd which is characteristic of paranoia as well as of Kafka's inventions, the nightmares that the insomniac Kafka would have suffered had he found sleep. As it was, he dreamed them during his nocturnal writing hours and narrated them in that wakefully sober and controlled prose that is so rare in German.

There can be no other novel so thoroughly pervaded by the sense of nightmare and paranoia as *The Trial*. "They [innocuous fellow lodgers in the boardinghouse] had perhaps been standing there all the time, they scrupulously avoided all appearance of having been observing him, they talked in low voices, following K.'s movements only with the abstracted gaze one has for people passing when one is deep in conversation. All the same, their glances weighed heavily upon K., and he made what haste he could to his room, keeping close against the wall." There is a plethora of such scenes in the novel: faces in windows across the street looking with intense curiosity into K.'s room; ears, real or imagined, pressed against doors; figures suddenly discovered standing and watching in the shadow of gateways; eyes peering through keyholes; defense lawyers who— "a possibility not to be excluded"—may secretly work for the defendant's accusers; rooms that had always

---

[4] Charles Baudelaire, *Oeuvres complètes*, Collection de la Pléiade (Paris, 1954, 1969), p. 519.

been presumed to be quite ordinary and that, upon inspection, reveal themselves as torture chambers. In the last instance, a man called Franz is being whipped, and K., detecting the horror, guiltily considers taking Franz's place. K. substituting for Franz: nobody initiated into Kafka's way with names will believe that Franz, one of the two warders of the Court who is now to be punished for having conducted himself reprehensibly when he arrested K., bears his author's name without purpose. It is the schizophrenia within, the laceration of identity, that outwardly becomes two persons, christened Franz and K., and thereby exorcised, just as the whole trial seems to be the perfect protective scheme designed by a paranoiac imagination. At every point it reflects the patient's contempt for the persecuting powers and at the same time his eagerness inwardly to bow to their authority; his persistent refusal to acknowledge any guilt on his part ("he admits that he doesn't know the Law and yet he claims he's innocent," Franz exclaims in the scene of the arrest in which K. finds himself incomprehensibly "decoyed into an exchange of speaking looks" with Franz); and, disastrously intermixed with this, his straining to imprison himself more and more in the cell of an unknown offense.

Torn as he was by the insoluble conflict between his self and the world, Kafka again and again tried to see F. B. as representing the world and that good life which is attained by "marrying, founding a family, accepting all the children that come": F. B., Felice Bauer, whose initials Kafka consistently used in the manuscript of *The Trial* for Fräulein Bürstner. This character's function in the fragmentary novel is utterly mysterious and particularly vexing because its great importance is never in doubt. Although it is said in one place, without apparent motivation, that "there is no connection between her and K.'s trial," we gather elsewhere that K.'s relationship with her—almost a blank in the fragments we have of the novel—"seems to fluctuate with the case itself." Her presence, fleeting and at this point even doubtful, is at its most ominous as K. is led to the quarry by his two executioners, who have interlocked their arms with his and hold his hands "in a methodical, practiced, irresistible grip." As the macabre group, "in a unity such as can hardly be formed except by lifeless matter,"[5] crosses the moonlit city square, "F. B. appeared. . . . It was not quite certain that it was she, but the resemblance was close enough." Upon seeing her, K. instantly "realized the futility of resistance." With K. now leading the way, all three follow her, not because he wants "to keep her in sight as long as possible, but only that he might not forget the lesson she had taught him." Now at last he accepts the verdict, and in the enforced company of the two silent men is grateful "that he has been allowed to say to himself all that is needed." The reader is not told what precisely it is that he does say to himself; but whatever it is, it means his acceptance of "the necessary," whether or not it is "the truth" (remembering what the Priest said in the Cathedral), and it is related to "the lesson" of F. B.

It is impossible to derive from the novel itself any exact notion of the "lesson," and thus of Joseph K.'s guilt, and thus of the meaning of *The Trial*. Lesson and guilt and meaning are inextricably enmeshed in the contradiction that is the gravitational center of Kafka's world: that the world of the senses is nothing but the Evil in the spiritual world, that at the same time one

[5] As his letters to Felice show, Kafka was fascinated by such "unities" and ways of interlocking arms and hands. See his 1913 New Year letter and the letter of February 14–15, 1913.

must "second" the "evil" world, choose the good life by marrying, having children, and doing cursed Adam's work in ploughing the fields—in short, live *dans le vrai*." Kafka was fond of quoting these words which Flaubert, his model martyr of literature, used of his niece's farming family, and there can be little doubt that the lesson Frl. B. has to teach Joseph K. is the same as the lesson Felice Bauer might have taught Kafka— at least in his obsessive suspicion: that he should have married her in order to live *dans le vrai*, even if that had meant ceasing to be a writer.

Or has "the lesson" and K.'s guilt anything to do, after all, with his betraying the pure world of the spirit by allowing his sensuality to draw him toward Fräulein Bürstner? The surmise is not entirely absurd. Only once before the terrible end when K. dies "like a dog!" did Kafka apply an animal metaphor to him: in the scene where, with the suddenness with which Kafka's "heroes" take the barrier between conversation and lovemaking, K. threw himself upon her, kissing her "all over the face, like some thirsty animal lapping greedily at a spring of long-sought fresh water." And the same assumption may draw support from Leni, the promiscuous woman who, upon meeting K., instantly seduces him and later proudly shows him her "physical defect": the connecting web of skin between two fingers of her right hand which is abnormally extended and reaches "almost to the top joint," linking her a little to creatures of the morass. But it is above all the story "The Judgment," intimately related to *The Trial* through F. B., to whom it is dedicated, that holds up this interpretation. There, as we have seen, the Father-Judge's fatal indictment of the son is based above all on his presumed sensual motivation in getting engaged to a "nasty creature." At both ends of the tension between the world of the senses and the world of the spirit there appears the greatest reluctance, indeed the incapacity, to resolve it.

All the same, one of Joseph K.'s "guilts" seems to weigh more heavily than the other: that he has "not yet eaten of the Tree of Life." As *The Trial* is undoubtedly the "mythological" offshoot of that Berlin *Gerichtshof*, the "Court of Law," the little gathering of relatives and friends before whom Kafka's engagement to F. B. was voided, and as Fräulein Bürstner is "mythologically" identical with Felice Bauer, it is surely permissible to turn to the letters Kafka wrote to Felice and to his diaries for a little help in comprehending the incomprehensible. Here, there is not the slightest trace of his reproaching himself for "sensual excess." The reverse is the case: his only relaxed and serene letters were written as the sequel of those summer days of 1916 in Marienbad when he and Felice, after some very unhappy days, lived together as lovers. After most other such sojourns he deplores in his diary the unbridgeable gulf between them, as he did on January 24, 1915. They had met in the Bohemian-German border town of Bodenbach, she having come there from Berlin, he from Prague. He read to her from his writings and she was bored; only during the reading of the legend "Before the Law" did she become more attentive. After the reading she said, *"Wie brav wir hier beisammen sind"* ("How well-behaved we are"), and he reports her words in the diary (January 24, 1915), confessing at the same time that they "haven't yet had a single good moment together," that with her "he never experienced (except in letters) that sweetness one experiences in a relationship with a woman one loves."

This virtuoso in inventing reasons for self-reproach does not once accuse himself in the secrecy of the diary of lacking sexual restraint in his relation with F. B.;

the reverse causes him moral discomfort—that he does not love and desire her enough when she is present. When it comes to the Tree of Life, Eve, it seems, does not easily succeed as seductress, and literature is the villain: it prevents him from living and stands between him and marriage to F. B. Yet if literature is his offense against life, it is at the same time—to join once more the viciously circular movements of Kafka's mind—the only, if vain, defense he can employ against the prosecution.

Kafka's descriptions, in *The Trial*, of the petitions K. sometimes intends to prepare to influence the Court in his favor almost always read like Kafka's diary reports of his terrible nocturnal struggles with words, or his maneuvers to wrest more time and energy for writing from his official duties. On one of his busy office mornings, Joseph K., so we read in the "Lawyer" section of Chapter VII, had suddenly pushed everything aside in order to draft such a plea, "but just at that moment the door of the Manager's room opened and the Assistant Manager came in laughing uproariously"—not at the plea, to be sure, but, like the demon of interruption that pursued Kafka's literary work, at a joke he wanted to share with K. But the petition

> simply had to be drawn up. If he could find no time for it in his office, which seemed very probable, then he must draft it in his lodgings by night. And if his nights were not enough, then he must ask for leave. . . . No doubt it was a task that meant almost interminable labor. One did not need to have a timid and fearful nature to be easily persuaded that the completion of this plea was a sheer impossibility . . . because to meet an unknown accusation . . . the whole of one's life would have to be recalled to mind, down to the

smallest actions and accidents, clearly formulated and examined from every angle.

Would he ever find his way through all these difficulties? Would not the writing of a thorough defense—"and any other kind would be a waste of time"—mean his cutting himself off from every other activity, and could he then live at all? This was not merely a matter of composing one petition, such as might be written during a short vacation from the office; no, what was involved was a whole *Prozess*, a process or trial of possibly endless duration. These are the exact questions that Kafka, with pained repetitiveness, asked himself in his diary or asked Felice.

During that night in which Kafka wrote "The Judgment" he felt, his diary records, that several times "I heaved my own weight on my back," and knew that "only *in this way* can writing be done." With his novel-writing, interrupted again and again, and stretching over years, he was, as we have heard him lament, "in the shameful lowlands of writing." Anyone having read and pondered these remarks cannot but think of them when the Lawyer in *The Trial* speaks to K. of two classes of lawyers (lawyers are, after all, the professional writers of "petitions" on behalf of the accused): the ordinary type who leads his client "by a slender thread until the verdict is reached," and the superior type who "lifts his client on his shoulders . . . and carries him without once letting him down until the verdict is reached, and even beyond it." (Where there is "verdict" in the English translation, there is *"Urteil"* in the German, "judgment." There is little doubt that Kafka thought of the story of that name.) Surely, the relations between Joseph K.'s trial and Kafka's writing could hardly be closer: literature belongs to the domain of that sin he has contracted, according to Kafka's aphorism, by eating only of the Tree of Knowledge, even if it is at the same time his only way of reaching out for the sphere of "the pure, the true, and the immutable," his way of praying.

Insofar as Kafka's art aims in *The Trial* at translating an inner state into a novel's sustained outward action—and be it the action of a busy nightmare—it fails, just as the tragedy of Oedipus, however elated its rhetoric and profound its insights, would be a failure if we were kept in ignorance about the guilt of the protagonist; just as the tragedy of Macbeth, however poignant its poetry, would break down if we were left wondering what on earth the poor man had done to earn his agonies; and this is so despite the incommensurable "otherness" of *The Trial*. Of course, the comparison is shockingly incongruous, yet the very shock of incongruity drives home the point: *The Trial* is Kafka's attempt to build a long narrative around guilt *as such*, without any explanation whence it comes; that is, around the resolution that later, in his "Reflections on Sin, Suffering, Hope, and the True Way," was expressed as "After this, never again psychology!"

After what? The preceding psychological "explanation," the kind of explanation that Kafka vows from now on is to be avoided, concerns the worship of idols, of "things," which, he says (in a manner reminiscent of Nietzsche), is rooted in the *fear* of things; or, rather, as he corrects himself (in a manner reminiscent only of Kafka), in "the fear of the necessity of things," which is nothing more or less than "the fear of responsibility for things." This surely implies the responsibility for the dichotomy between the I and "things," for the enmity between the I and the external world, for the deadly conflict between the spiritual realm and the domain of the senses; that is, for the Fall. Having reached this terminus, albeit by means of psychological intuition, psychology is left behind. Yet a novel cannot leave psychology behind (despite some theorists of the *nouveau roman*). He who transcended psychology also transcended the literary form of the novel. At Kafka's hands novels were bound to remain fragmentary. Bertolt Brecht proved to be a perspicacious critic when he spoke to Walter Benjamin of Kafka's ultimate failure as a novelist.[6] He failed, Brecht said, because he was meant to be what Confucius was: he had the disposition and gift of a great teacher, but, as there was for Kafka no society to teach or prophetically to inspire, his Confucian parables illegitimately became "literature," "mere" literature. ("If I were a Chinese . . ." Kafka once wrote to Felice [May 1916], and added, "Indeed I am a Chinese.") The prophetic parables grew into "art," even into abortive novels, and thus lost their parabolic consistency and seriousness. "They were never quite transparent," said Brecht. This is also the reason why the apparent precision of Kafka's style is so deceptive: it is the precision of an exact dream confusingly dreamt in a place between prophecy and art.

It remains the great virtue of Kafka's failure that he presents guilt as an *Urphänomen*, an irreducible phenomenon. Within the world of *The Trial* guilt has no legal content or sufficient psychological cause. It is, for Kafka, part of the anatomy of the soul, just as is the impossible search of the restlessly homeless mind in *The Castle*.

[6] Walter Benjamin, *Versuche über Brecht* (Frankfurt am Main, 1966), pp. 119*ff.*

The Castle

iv

I

The relationship of Kafka's heroes to that truth
for which they so desperately search can best be
seen in the image through which Plato, in a
famous passage of his *Republic*, expresses man's
pitiable ignorance about the true nature of the
Ideas. Chained to the ground of his cave, with
his back toward the light, all man perceives of
the fundamental reality of the world is a play of
shadows thrown on to the wall of his prison. But
for Kafka there is a further complication: perfectly aware of his wretched imprisonment and
obsessed with a monomaniac desire to know, the
prisoner has by his unruly behavior and his incessant entreaties provoked the government of
his prison to an act of malicious generosity. In
order to satisfy his passion for knowledge they

have covered the walls with mirrors which, owing to the curved surface of the cave, distort what they reflect. Now the prisoner sees lucid pictures, definite shapes, clearly recognizable faces, an inexhaustible wealth of detail. His gaze is fixed no longer on empty shades but on a full reflection of ideal reality. Face to face with the images of Truth, he is yet doubly agonized by their hopeless distortion. With an unparalleled fury of pedantry he observes the curve of every line, the ever-changing countenance of every figure, drawing schemes of every possible aberration from reality which his mirror may cause, making now this angle and now that the basis of his endless calculations, which, he passionately hopes, will finally yield the geometry of truth or of that necessity which sometimes he opposed to the notion of truth.

In his diary (December 16, 1911) Kafka says, "I am separated from all things by a hollow space, and I do not even reach to its boundaries." In another entry (November 19 and 21, 1913): "Everything appears to me construed. . . . I am chasing after constructions. I enter a room, and I find them in a corner, a white tangle." On October 21, 1921, he enters: "All is imaginary—family, office, friends, the street, all imaginary, far away or close at hand, the woman; the truth that lies closest, however, is only this, that you are beating your head against the wall of a windowless and doorless cell." And in one of his "Reflections on Sin, Pain, Hope, and the True Way" he says, "Our art is a dazzled blindness before the truth: the light on the grotesque recoiling mask is true, but nothing else."

Kafka's novels take place in infinity. Yet their atmosphere is as oppressive as that of those unaired rooms in which so many of their scenes are enacted. For infinity is incompletely defined as the ideal point where two parallels meet. There is yet another place where they come together: the distorting mirror. Thus they carry into the prison of their violently distorted union the agony of infinite separation.

It is a Tantalus situation, and in Kafka's work the ancient curse has come to life once more. Kafka says of himself (in the sequence of aphorisms "He," contained in the volume *The Great Wall of China*), "He is thirsty, and is cut off from a spring by a mere clump of bushes. But he is divided against himself: one part overlooks the whole, sees that he is standing here and that the spring is just beside him; but another part notices nothing, has at most a divination that the first part sees all. But as he notices nothing he cannot drink." Indeed, it was a curse, and not a word of light, which called the universe of Kafka's novels into existence. The very clay from which it was made bore the imprint of a malediction before the creator had touched it. He builds to a splendid design, but the curse runs like a vein through every stone. In one of his most revealing parables, in the Fourth Octavo Note-Book (included in the volume *Dearest Father*), Kafka shows himself aware of this:

> Everything fell in with his intention and contributed to the building. Foreign workers brought the blocks of marble, already hewn and ready to be fitted together. In accordance with the indication, given by his moving finger, the blocks rose up and shifted into place. No building ever rose into being as easily as this temple did, or rather, this temple came into being in the true manner of temples. Only on every block—from what quarry did they come?—there were clumsy scribblings by senseless childish hands, or rather, entries made by barbaric mountain-dwellers in order to annoy or to deface or to destroy completely, scratched into the stone

with instruments that were obviously magnificently sharp, intended to endure for an eternity that would outlast the temple.

It is the reality of the curse that constitutes the ruthlessly compelling logic of Kafka's writings. If they defy all attempts to interpret them in a simple, straightforward manner, this is because he never thinks, or imagines, in disputable or refutable generalities. His thinking is a reflex movement of his being and shares the irrefutability of all that is. It is at an infinite number of removes from the Cartesian *cogito ergo sum*. Indeed, it sometimes seems that an unknown "It" does all the thinking that matters, the radius of its thought touching the circumference of his existence here and there, causing him infinite pain, bringing his life into question and promising salvation on one condition only: that he should expand his being to bring it within the orbit of that strange Intelligence. The formula has become: "It thinks, and therefore I am not," with only the agony of despair providing overpowering proof that he is alive.

There is, outside this agony, no reality about which Kafka could entertain or communicate thoughts, nothing apart from the curse of his own separation from that Intelligence. Yet a complete world is to be found within that pain, the exact pattern of creation once more, but this time made of the stuff of which curses are made. Like sorrow in the Tenth of Rilke's *Duino Elegies*, despair is given a home of its own in Kafka's works, faithfully made in the image of customary life, but animated by the blast of the curse. This gives to Kafka's writings their unique quality. Never before has absolute darkness been represented with so much clarity, and the very madness of desperation with so much composure and sobriety. In his works an intolerable spiritual pride is

expressed with the convincing gesture of humility, dis-
integration finds its own level of integrity and impenetrable complexity an all but *sancta simplicitas*. Kafka
strives to discover the moral law of a boundlessly deceit-
ful world, and performs in a totally incalculable domain,
ruled by evil demons, the most precise mathematical
measurements.

It has been said that *The Castle* is a religious allegory,
a kind of modern *Pilgrim's Progress*; that the unattainable building is the abode of divine law and divine grace.
This would seem to be a misapprehension reflecting a
profound religious confusion, a loss of all sureness of
religious discrimination. Where there is a spiritual
famine, *anything* that is of the spirit may taste like
bread from Heaven, and minds imbued with psychology
and "comparative religion" may find the difference negligible between Prometheus, clamped to the rock, and
the martyrdom of a Christian saint; between an ancient
curse and the grace that makes a new man.

The Castle is as much a religious allegory as a photo-
graphic likeness of the devil in person could be said to
be an allegory of Evil. Every allegory has an opening
into the rarefied air of abstractions and is furnished
with signposts pointing to an ideal concept beyond. But
The Castle is a terminus of soul and mind, a *non plus
ultra* of existence. In an allegory the author plays a
kind of guessing game with his reader, if he does not
actually provide the answers himself; but there is no
key to *The Castle*. It is true that its reality does not
precisely correspond to what is commonly understood in
the "positive" world as real, namely, neutral sense per-
ceptions of objects and, neatly separated from them,
feelings (hence our most authentic and realistic intellectual pursuits—natural sciences and psychology; and
our besetting sins—the ruthlessness of acquisitive tech-

niques and sentimentality). In Kafka's novels there is no such division between the external sphere and the domain of inwardness, and therefore no such reality. There is only the tragic mythology of the absolutely incongruous relationship between the two worlds.

Kafka's creations are at the opposite pole to the writings of that type of romantic poet, the true poetical representative of the utilitarian age, who distills from a spiritually more and more sterile external reality those elements which are still of some use to the passions, or else withdraws from its barren fields into the greenhouse vegetation of inwardness. The author of *The Castle* does not select for evocative purposes, nor does he project his inner experience into carefully chosen timeless settings. Kafka does not, after the manner of Joyce, give away, in the melodious flow of intermittent articulation, the secret bedroom conversations which self conducts with self. There are no private symbols in his work, such as would be found in symbolist writing, no crystallized fragments of inner sensations charged with mysterious significance; nor is there, after the fashion of the expressionists, any rehearsing of new gestures of the soul, meant to be more in harmony with the new rhythm of modern society. Instead of all this, the reader is faced with the shocking spectacle of a miraculously sensitive soul incapable of being either reasonable or cynical or resigned or rebellious about the prospect of eternal damnation. The world which this soul perceives is unmistakably "real," a castle that is a castle and "symbolizes" merely what all castles symbolize: power and authority; a bureaucracy drowning in a deluge of forms and files; an obscure hierarchy of officialdom making it impossible ever to find the man authorized to deal with a particular case; officials who work overtime and yet get nowhere; numberless interviews which never are to the point; inns where the peasants meet, and barmaids who serve the officials. In fact, it is an excruciatingly familiar world, but reproduced by a creative intelligence endowed with the knowledge that it is a world damned forever. Shakespeare once made one of his characters say: "They say miracles are past; and we have our philosophical persons, to make modern and familiar, things supernatural and causeless. Hence it is that we make trifles of terrors; ensconcing ourselves in seeming knowledge, when we should submit ourselves to an unknown fear." In Kafka we have the abdication of the philosophical persons.

In his work the terror recaptures the trifles, and the unknown fear invades all seeming knowledge—particularly that of psychology. Even the most mistaken religious interpretations of Kafka's writings show at least an awareness of their author's spirit whereas the psychological analyses, in their devastating plausibility, tend to reduce them to symptoms of the Oedipus complex. Certainly, there cannot be the slightest doubt that Kafka's relationship to his father was exceedingly strained; but only one son, among the many unable to come to terms with their fathers, has written *The Castle*. To interpret this or any other novel of Kafka's in the perspective of the Oedipus complex is about as helpful to our understanding of his work as the statement that Kafka would have been a different person (and perhaps not a writer at all) if he had had another father: a thought which even psychologically less initiated ages might have been capable of if they had deemed it worth thinking. This kind of psychology can contribute as much to the explanation of a work of art as ornithological anatomy to the comprehension of what the nightingale's song meant to Keats. But so deeply ingrained is psychology in the epoch's sensibility that most readers, even when they are moved by the symbolic reality which the author has created, soon regain the balance of mind required for the translation of the symbol into what it "really" means; and by that they mean precisely that meaningless experience which the artist has succeeded in transcending through his poetic creation. If, for instance, the writer believes he has discovered the meaning of his senselessly tormenting feud with his father (a discovery he has made in creating his work)—that he should find his place within a true spiritual order of divine authority—the psychological reader will insist that the author "really" means his father.

In Kafka we have the modern mind, seemingly self-sufficient, intelligent, skeptical, ironical, splendidly trained for the great game of pretending that the world it comprehends in sterilized sobriety is the only and ultimate real one—yet a mind living in sin with the soul of Abraham. Thus he knows two things at once, and both with equal assurance: that there is no God, and that there must be God. It is the perspective of the curse: the intellect dreaming its dream of absolute freedom, and the soul knowing of its terrible bondage. The conviction of damnation is all that is left of faith, standing out like a rock in a landscape the softer soil of which has been eroded by the critical intellect. Kafka once said (in the Fourth Octavo Note-Book): "I should welcome eternity, and when I do find it I am sad."

This is merely an exhausted echo of the fanfares of despair with which Nietzsche, who had some share in Kafka's intellectual education and is, beyond any question of influence, in many respects one of his spiritual ancestors, welcomed his vision of eternity. In one of the posthumously published notes on *Zarathustra* Nietzsche says about his idea of the Eternal Recurrence: "We have produced the hardest possible thought—now let us create the creature who will accept it lightheartedly and blissfully!" the *Übermensch*. He conceived the Eternal Recurrence as a kind of spiritualized Darwinian test to select for survival the spiritually fittest. This he formulated with the utmost precision: "I perform the great experiment: who can bear the idea of Eternal Recurrence?" (XIV, 179) We gain an ever-deeper insight into the anatomy of despair from Nietzsche's posthumous aphorisms and epigrams which were assembled by his editors in the two volumes of *The Will to Power*, many of which refer to the idea of Eternal Recurrence: "Let us consider this idea in its most terrifying form: existence, as it is, without meaning or goal, but inescapably recurrent, without a finale into nothingness. . . ." (XVIII, 45) Nietzsche's *Übermensch* is the creature strong enough to live a cursed existence forever, even to derive from it the Dionysian raptures of tragic acceptance. Nietzsche feels certain that only the *Übermensch* could be equal to the horror of a senseless eternity and perform the great metamorphosis of turning this "most terrifying" knowledge into the terror of superhuman delight. And Kafka? On most of the few occasions when he mentions happiness in his diary he registers it as the result of a transformation of torture into bliss as in those horrible diary entries already quoted, of which one (November 2, 1911) is: "This morning, for the first time in a long time, the joy again of imagining a knife twisted in my heart." If Nietzsche's *Übermensch* is the visionary counterweight to the weight of the curse, then Kafka is its chosen victim. What sometimes has been interpreted as signs of a religious "breakthrough" in his later writings, is merely the all-engulfing weariness of a Nietzschean Prometheus. In the fourth of his Prometheus legends (Fourth Octavo Note-Book) Kafka writes: ". . . everyone grew weary of the meaningless affair. The gods grew weary, the eagles grew weary, the wound closed wearily."

Thus Kafka's work, as much as Nietzsche's, must remain a stumbling block to the analyzing interpreter to whom, in the enlightened atmosphere of modernity, the word "curse" comes only as a faint memory of Greek tragedy, or as a figurative term for a combination of ill-luck and psychological maladjustments. Yet the gray world of Kafka's novels is luminous with its fire. To be sure, Kafka's *Castle* is, as has been maintained, about life in the grip of a power "which all religions have acknowledged"; but this power is not "divine law and divine grace," but rather one which, having rebelled against the first and fallen from the second, has, in its own domain, successfully contrived the suspension of both. Undoubtedly, the Land Surveyor K., hero of *The Castle*, is religiously fascinated by its inscrutably horrid bureaucracy; but again it is a word from Nietzsche, and not from the Gospels, that sums up the situation: "Wretched man, your god lies in the dust, broken to fragments, and serpents dwell around him. And now you love even the serpents for his sake" (XIV, 80).

2

The Castle is not an allegorical, but a symbolic novel. A discussion of the difference could easily deteriorate into pedantry, the more so as, in common and literary usage, the terms are applied rather arbitrarily. It will, however, help our understanding of Kafka's work if we distinguish, in using these two terms, two different modes of experience and expression. I shall therefore define my own use of these words.

The symbol is what it represents; the allegory represents what, in itself, it is *not*. The terms of reference of an allegory are abstractions; a symbol refers to something specific and concrete. The statue of a blindfolded woman, holding a pair of scales, is an *allegory* of Justice; bread and wine are, for the Christian communicant, *symbols* of the Body and Blood of Christ.[1] Thus an allegory must always be rationally translatable; whether a symbol is translatable or not depends on the fundamental agreement of society on the question of what kind of experience, out of the endless range of possible human experience, it regards as significant. The possibility of allegorizing will only vanish with the last man capable of *thinking in abstractions* and of forming *images* of them; yet the validity of symbols depends not on rational operations but on complex experiences in which thought and feeling merge in the act of spiritual comprehension. The sacramental symbols, for instance, would become incommunicable among a race of men who no longer regard the life, death, and resurrection of Christ as spiritually relevant *facts*. An allegory, being the imaginary representation of something abstract, is, as it were, doubly unreal: whereas the symbol, in being what it represents, possesses a double reality.

Goethe, summing up in one line at the end of *Faust II* the mature wisdom of his life, attributes whatever permanent reality there may be in a transient world to its symbolic significance. What is, is only *real* insofar as it is symbolic. Earlier in his life he defined the "true symbol" as that "particular" which represents the "universal," not, however, "as a dream or shadow, but as the

[1] I should like to beg the indulgence of the reader for disregarding the established theological terminology. The following discussion will, I hope, to some extent justify my apparent arbitrariness, which I do not wish to maintain outside the scope of this particular argument.

revelation of the unfathomable in a moment filled with life."[2]

The predicament of the symbol in our age is caused by a split between "reality" and what it signifies. There is no more any commonly accepted symbolic or transcendent order of things. What the modern mind perceives as order is established through the tidy relationship between things themselves. In one word: the only conceivable order is positivist-scientific. If there still is a—no doubt, diminishing—demand for the fuller reality of the symbol, then it must be provided for by the unsolicited gifts of art. But in the sphere of art the symbolic substance, dismissed from its disciplined commitments to reality, dissolves into incoherence, ready to attach itself to any fragment of experience, invading it with irresistible power, so that a pair of boots, or a chair in the painter's attic, or a single tree on a slope which the poet passes, or an obscure inscription in a Venetian church, may suddenly become the precariously unstable center of an otherwise unfocused universe. Since "the great words, from the time when what really happened was still visible, are no longer for us" (as Rilke put it in his "Requiem for a Young Poet"), the "little words" have to carry an excessive freight of symbolic significance. No wonder that they are slow in delivering it. They are all but incommunicable private symbols, established beyond any doubt as symbols by the quality and intensity of the imaginative experience that has brought them forth, but lacking any representative properties. Such is the economy of human consciousness that the positivist impoverishment of the one region produces anarchy in the other. In the end, atomic lawlessness is likely to prevail in both.

[2] *Maximen und Reflexionen*, No. 314 (in the widely accepted numbering of Max Hecker's edition), (Weimar, 1907).

The intellectual foundation of every human society is a generally accepted model of reality. One of the major intellectual difficulties of human existence seems to be due to the fact that this model of reality is in every case a mere *interpretation* of the world, and yet it exerts, as long as it seems the valid interpretation, the subtly compelling claim to being accepted as the only true picture of the universe, indeed as truth itself. This difficulty, manifesting itself in the deeper strata of doubt by which certain intellectually sensitive men have been affected, develops easily into a mental epidemic in epochs in which a certain model of reality crumbles and collapses. It seems that we have lived in such an epoch for a long time. One of its main characteristics has been the uncertainty, steadily increasing in the minds and feelings of men, about the relation between mundane and transcendental reality, or, in other words, about the meaning of life and death, the destiny of the soul, the nature and sanction of moral laws, and the relative domains of knowledge and faith.

Insofar as Christianity was the representative religion of the Middle Ages, their model of reality was essentially sacramental. A definite correspondence prevailed between the mundane and transcendental spheres. Faith was not established in any distinct "religious experience," nor as a particular "mode of comprehension," kept apart from "knowledge." It was an element in *all* experience, indeed its crystallizing principle. Only within a mold and pattern determined by faith did experiences make sense and impressions turn to knowledge. This correspondence between the two spheres was so close that at every important stage of a man's life they met and became one in the sacraments.

The sacramental model of reality, intermittently disputed and questioned throughout the whole development

of Christian theological thought, was upset in a histori-
cally decisive fashion at the time of the Reformation.
During that period an intellectual tension, inherent in
Christian dogma, developed into a conflagration of vast
historical consequences. It produced an articulate climax
—which was, however, a mere symptom of a more inarticulate, yet more comprehensive process—at a particularly exposed point of dogmatic faction: the sacramental dispute between Luther and Zwingli. Luther,
despite his divergent interpretation of the traditional
dogma, represents in it the essentially medieval view,
whereas Zwingli, disciple of the humanist Pico della
Mirandola, is the spokesman of modernity. To Luther
the sacrament of the Last Supper is Christ (the bread
and the wine *are* what they represent), while Zwingli
reduces it to the status of an allegory (as merely representing what, in itself, it is not). From then onward the
word "merely" has been attaching itself ever more firmly
to the word "symbol," soon gaining sufficient strength
to bring about a complete estrangement between the two
spheres. A new order of things finally emerged. Within
it the transcendental realm is allotted the highest honors
of the spirit, but at the same time skillfully deprived of a
considerable measure of reality; the mundane, on the
other hand, is compensated for its lowering in spiritual
stature by the chance of absorbing all available reality
and becoming more "really" real than before.

The sudden efflorescence of physical science in the
seventeenth century is the positive result of this sever-
ance. Its successes have further contributed to the
"lower realm" setting itself up as the only "really" real
one, and as the sole provider of relevant truth, order,
and lawfulness. Scientific and other positivist pursuits
owe the unchallenged dominion which they have en-
joyed ever since over the intellectual life of Europe to

the ever more exclusive fascination which the new model of reality has had for the European mind.

As an unavoidable corollary of this state of affairs, religion and art lost their unquestioned birthright in the homeland of human reality and turned into strange messengers from the higher unreality, admitted now and then as edifying or entertaining songsters at the positivist banquet. What had once been a matter-of-fact expression of life became a "problem," worthy of a great deal of intellectual fuss and a negligible assignment of reality. As far as the arts are concerned, it is most revealing that the only *distinctive* artistic achievement of Europe since the end of the seventeenth century was accomplished by the art with the least claim to "reality": music, while the most "real" of all arts, architecture, degenerated until it gained new vitality as the unashamed functional servant of technology.

In Germany, a country which, for historical reasons too complex ever to be unraveled, suddenly rose in the eighteenth century, without any gradual transition from the Middle Ages, to the heights of European consciousness and to the fulfillment of the most extravagant intellectual aspirations, the plight of the poet within the new model of reality is most conspicuous. The artist as an exile from reality is one of the most authentic themes of German literature, from Goethe's *Torquato Tasso* and Grillparzer's *Sappho* to Thomas Mann's *Tonio Kröger*. Kleist, Hölderlin, Nietzsche are the greatest among the victims of a hopeless collision between, on the one hand, the demand for a realization of the spirit within the reality of the world and, on the other, the inexorable resistance of a safely established spirit-proof view of life. Hölderlin is the greatest poet among these involuntary desperadoes of the spirit. His work is one continuous attempt to recapture the lost reality of the symbol and the sacramental experience of life. And for Goethe, to preserve his life, exposed at every point to the revengeful blows of the banished spirit, was, from beginning to end, a struggle, entailing the most precarious maneuvers of compromise, irony, and resignation. It was only—ironically enough—in his scientific activities that he gave vent to his unrestrained anger at the analytical-positivist view of the world and its scientific exposition through mathematics and Newtonian physics. How gloriously he blundered into physical science, determined to meet the enemy on his own ground, and how stubbornly convinced he was of being right! He once said to Eckermann (February 19, 1829): "Whatever I have achieved as a poet is nothing to be particularly proud of. Excellent poets are my contemporaries, still better poets lived before me, and others will come after me. But in my own century I am the only man who knows what is right in the difficult science of colors; and this is something that gives me real satisfaction and a feeling of superiority over many." His own idea of science was based upon the *Urphänomen*, a striking assertion of the symbol as the final and irreducible truth of reality.

Goethe lost the battle for the symbol. In the century that stretches between his death and Kafka's writing, reality was all but completely sealed off against any transcendental intrusion. In Kafka's work the symbolic substance, forced back in every attempt to attack from above, invades reality from down below, carrying with it the stuff from Hell. Or it need not even invade: Kafka writes at the point where the world, having become too heavy with spiritual emptiness, begins to sink into the unsuspected demon-ridden depths of unbelief. In this cataclysm, the more disastrous because it overtakes a world which has not even believed in its own unbelief, Kafka's heroes struggle in vain for spiritual survival. Thus his creations are symbolic, for they are infused with, and not merely allegorical of, negative transcendence.

Kafka knew the symbolic or parabolic nature of his work; he knew, too, of the complete alienation of modern man from the reality of the symbol. The following is one of his profoundest meditations. It is called "On Parables" (included in *The Complete Stories*). The German is *"Gleichnisse,"* and "symbols" would have been—in this case—an equally fitting translation:

Many complain that the words of the wise are always merely parables and of no use in daily life, which is the only life we have. When the wise man says: "Go over," he does not mean that we should cross to some actual place, which we could do anyhow if the labor were worth it; he means some fabulous yonder, something unknown to us, something that he too cannot designate more precisely either, and therefore help us here in the very least. All these parables really set out to say merely that the incomprehensible is incomprehensible, and we know that already. But the cares we have to struggle with every day: that is a different matter.

Concerning this a man once said: Why such reluctance? If you only followed the parables you yourselves would become parables and with that rid of all your daily cares.

Another said: I bet this is also a parable.

The first said: You have won.

The second said: But unfortunately only in parable.

The first said: No, in reality; in parable you have lost.

3

There are, however, allegorical elements to be found in *The Castle*: for instance, the names of many of the characters. The hero himself, who is introduced with the bare initial K. (undoubtedly once again an autobiographical hint—the novel was originally drafted in the first person—and at the same time, through its very incompleteness, suggesting an unrealized, almost anonymous personality), is a Land Surveyor. Kafka's choice of this profession for his hero clearly has a meaning. The German for it is *Landvermesser*, and its verbal associations are manifold. The first is, of course, the Land Surveyor's professional activity, consisting precisely in what K. desperately desires and never achieves: to produce a workable order within clearly defined boundaries and limits of earthly life, and to find an acceptable compromise between conflicting claims of possession. But *Vermesser* also alludes to *Vermessenheit*, hubris; to the adjective *vermessen*, audacious; to the verb *sich vermessen*, to commit an act of spiritual pride, *and* also to apply the wrong measure, make a mistake in measurement. The most powerful official of the Castle (for K. the highest representative of authority) is called Klamm, a sound producing a sense of anxiety amounting almost to claustrophobia, suggesting pincers, chains, clamps, but also a person's oppressive silence. The messenger of the Castle (as it turns out later, self-appointed and officially never recognized) has the name of Barnabas, the same as that man of Cyprus who, though not one of the Twelve, came to rank as an apostle; "Son of Consolation," or "Son of Exhortation," is the Biblical meaning of his name, and it is said that his exhortation was of the inspiring kind, and so built up faith. And the Barnabas of the novel is indeed a son of consolation, if only in the desperately ironical sense that his family, whom the curse of the Castle has cast into the lowest depths of misery and wretchedness, in vain expects deliverance through his voluntary service for the authority. To K., however, his messages, in all their obscurity and pointlessness, seem the only real link with the Castle, an elusive glimmer of hope, a will-o'-the-wisp of faith. Barnabas's counterpart is Momus, the village secretary of Klamm and namesake of that depressing creature, the son of Night, whom the Greek gods authorized to find fault with all things. In the novel it is he whose very existence seems the denial of any hope which Barnabas may have roused in K. Frieda (peace) is the girl through whose love K. seeks to reach the goal of his striving; Bürgel (diminutive of *Bürge*, guarantor) is the name of the little official who offers the solution without K.'s even noticing the chance; and the secretary, through whom K. does expect to achieve something and achieves nothing, is called Erlanger (citizen of the town of Erlangen, but also suggestive of *erlangen*, to attain, achieve).

This discussion of names provides an almost complete synopsis of the slender plot of *The Castle*. Someone, a man whose name begins with K., and of whom we know no more, neither whence he comes nor what his past life has been, arrives in a village which is ruled by a Castle. He believes that he has been appointed Land Surveyor by the authorities. The few indirect contacts that K. succeeds in establishing with the Castle—a letter he receives, a telephone conversation he overhears, yet another letter, and above all the fact that he is joined by two assistants whom the rulers have assigned to him —*seem* to confirm his appointment. Yet he himself is never quite convinced, and he never relaxes in his efforts to ascertain it. He feels he must penetrate to the very center of authority and wring from it a kind of ultra-final confirmation of his claim. Until then he yields, in paralyzed despair, broken by only momentary outbursts of rebellious pride, to the inarticulate yet absolutely self-assured refusal of the village to acknowledge him as their Land Surveyor: "You've been taken on as Land Surveyor, as you say, but, unfortunately, we have no need of a Land Surveyor. There wouldn't be the least use for one here. The frontiers of our little estates are marked out and all officially recorded. So what should we do with a Land Surveyor?" (V) says the village representative to him.

K.'s belief appears, from the very outset, to be based on both truth and illusion. It is Kafka's all but unbeliev-able achievement to force, indeed to frighten, the reader into unquestioning acceptance of this paradox, presented with ruthless realism and irresistible logic. Truth and illusion are mingled in such a way in K.'s belief that he is deprived of all order of reality. Truth is permanently on the point of taking off its mask and revealing itself as illusion, illusion in constant danger of being verified as truth. It is the predicament of a man who, endowed with an insatiable appetite for the absolute certainty that transcends all half-truths, relativities, and com-promises of everyday life, finds himself in a world robbed of all spiritual possessions. Thus he cannot ac-cept the world—the village—without first attaining to that certainty, and he cannot be certain without first accepting the world. Yet every contact with the world makes a mockery of his search, and the continuance of his search turns the world into a mere encumbrance. After studying the first letter from the Castle, K. con-templates his dilemma, "whether he preferred to become a village worker with a distinctive but merely apparent connection with the Castle, or an ostensible village worker whose real occupation was determined through the medium of Barnabas" (I). From the angle of the village, all K.'s contacts with the Castle are figments of his imagination: "You haven't once up till now come into real contact with our authorities. All those contacts have been illusory, but owing to your ignorance of the circumstances you take them to be real" (V). The Castle, on the other hand, seems to take no notice whatever of the reality of K.'s miserable village existence. In the midst of his suffering the indignity of being employed as a kind of footman to the schoolmaster, and never having come anywhere near working as a Land Surveyor, he receives the following letter from Klamm: "The surveying work which you have carried out thus far has been appreciated by me. . . . Do not slacken in your efforts! Carry your work to a fortunate conclusion. Any interruption would displease me. . . . I shall not forget you" (X). From all this it would appear that it is, in fact, the village that disobeys the will of the Castle, while defeating K. with the powerful suggestion that he misunderstands the intentions of authority. And yet the authority seems to give its blessing to the defiance of the village and to punish K. for his determination to act in accordance with the letter of its orders. In his fanatical obedience it is really he who rebels against the Castle, whereas the village, in its matter-of-fact refusal, lives the life of the Law.

Kafka represents the absolute reversal of German idealism. If it is Hegel's final belief that in the Absolute truth and existence are one, for Kafka it is precisely through the Absolute that they are forever divided. Truth and existence are mutually exclusive. From his early days it was the keenest wish of Kafka the artist to convey this in works of art; to write in such a way that life, in all its deceptively convincing reality, would be seen as a dream and a nothing before the Absolute: ". . . somewhat as if one were to hammer together a table with painful and methodical technical efficiency, and simultaneously do nothing at all, and not in such a way that people could say: 'Hammering a table together is nothing to him,' but rather 'Hammering a table together is really hammering a table together to him, but at the same time it is nothing,' whereby certainly the hammering would have become still bolder, still surer, still more real and, if you will, still more senseless." This is how Kafka, in the series of aphorisms "He," describes the vision of artistic accomplishment which hovered before his mind's eye when, as a young man, he sat one day on the slopes of the Laurenziberg in Prague. Has he, in his later works, achieved this artistic justification of nonentity? Not quite: what was meant to become the lifting of a curse through art, became the artistically perfect realization of it, and what he dreamed of making into something as light as a dream, fell from his hands with the heaviness of a nightmare. Instead of a vindication of nothingness, he achieved the portrayal of the most cunningly vindictive unreality.

It is hard to understand how *The Castle* could possibly be called a religious allegory with a pilgrim of the type of Bunyan's as its hero. Pilgrimage? On the contrary, the most oppressive quality of Kafka's work is the unshakable stability of its central situation. It takes place in a world that knows of no motion, no change, no metamorphosis—unless it be the transformation of a human being into an insect. Its caterpillars never turn into butterflies, and when the leaves of a tree tremble it is not due to the wind: it is the stirring of a serpent coiled round its branches. Pilgrim or not, there is no progress to be watched in *The Castle*, unless we agree to call progress what Kafka describes in "A Little Fable" as the "progress" of the mouse: " 'Alas,' said the mouse, 'the world is growing smaller every day. At the beginning it was so big that I was afraid, I kept running and running, and I was glad when at last I saw walls far away to the right and left, but these long walls have narrowed so quickly that I am in the last chamber already, and there in the corner stands the trap that I must run into.' 'You only need to change your direction,' said the cat, and ate it up." It has been said that Kafka has this in common with Bunyan, "that the goal and the road indubitably exist, and that the necessity to find them is urgent." Only the second point is correct. Indeed, so urgent is it for Kafka to discover the road and reach the goal that life seems impossible without this achievement. But do road and goal exist? "There is a goal, but no way; what we call the way is only wavering," is what Kafka says about it in "Reflections on Sin, Suffering, Hope, and the True Way." And is there really a goal for him? This is the answer that Kafka gives to himself in "He": "He feels imprisoned on this earth, he feels constricted; the melancholy, the impotence, the sickness, the feverish fancies of the captive afflict him; no comfort can comfort him, since it is merely comfort, gentle head-splitting comfort glozing the brutal fact of imprisonment. But if he is asked what he actually wants he cannot reply, for—that is one of his strongest proofs —he has no conception of freedom."

Kafka's hero is the man who *believes* in absolute freedom but cannot have any conception of it because he *exists* in a world of slavery. Therefore it is not grace and salvation that he seeks, but either his right or a bargain with the powers. "I don't want any act of favor from the Castle, but my rights" (V), says K. in his interview with the village representative. But convinced of the futility of this expectation, his real hope is based on Frieda, his fiancée and Klamm's former mistress, whom K. is obviously prepared to hand back to him "for a price."

In K.'s relationship to Frieda the European story of romantic love has found its epilogue. It is the solid residue left behind by the evaporated perfume of romance, revealing its darkest secret. In romantic love, as it has dominated a vast section of European literature ever since the later Middle Ages, individualism, emerging from the ruins of a common spiritual order, has found its most powerful means of transcendence. The spiritually more and more autonomous (therefore more and more lonely) individual worships Eros and his twin deity within the romantic imagination, Death, as the only gods capable of breaking down the barriers of his individualist isolation. Therefore love becomes tragedy: overcharged with unmanageable spiritual demands it needs must surge ahead of any human relationship. In its purest manifestations, romantic love is a glorious disaster of the soul, carrying frustration in its wake. For what the romantic lover seeks is not really the beloved. Intermixed with his erotic craving, inarticulate, diffuse, and yet dominating it, is the desire for spiritual salvation. Even a "happy ending" spells profound disillusionment for the romantic expectation. Perhaps it is Strindberg, deeply admired by Kafka, who wrote the last chapter of its history. It is certainly Kafka who wrote its postscript.

For K. loves Frieda—if he loves her at all—entirely for Klamm's sake. This is not only implied in the whole story of K. and Frieda, but explicitly stated by Kafka in several passages that he later deleted, probably because their directness seemed to him incompatible with the muted meaning of the book. As an indictment of K., it is contained in the protocol about his life in the village which Momus has drawn up, and in which K. is accused of having made up to Frieda out of a "calculation of the lowest sort": because he believed that in her he would win a mistress of Klamm's and so possess "a pledge for which he can demand the highest price." On the margin of the protocol there was also "a childishly scrawled drawing, a man with a girl in his arms. The girl's face was buried in the man's chest, but the man, who was much the taller, was looking over the girl's shoulders at a sheet of paper he had in his hands and on which he was joyfully inscribing some figures." But perhaps still more conclusive than Momus's clearly hostile interpretation is another deleted passage giving K.'s own reflections on his love for Frieda:

And then immediately, before there was any time to think, Frieda had come, and with her the belief, which it was impossible to give up entirely even today, that through her mediation an almost physical relationship to Klamm, a relationship so close that it amounted almost to a whispering form of communication, had come about, of which for the present only K. knew, which however needed only a little intervention, a word, a glance, in order to reveal itself primarily to Klamm, but then too to everyone, as something admittedly incredible which was nevertheless, through the compulsion of life, the compulsion of the loving embrace, a matter of course. . . . What . . . was he without Frieda? A nonentity, staggering along after . . . will-o'-the-wisps. . . .[3]

The desperate desire for spiritual certainty is all that is left of romantic love. K. *wills* his love for Frieda be-

---

[3] The deleted passages are published in the Appendix of the definitive edition of *The Castle.*

cause he *wills* his salvation.[4] He is a kind of Pelagius believing that he "can if he ought," yet living in a relentlessly predestined world. This situation produces a theology very much after the model of Gnostic and Manichaean beliefs. The incarnation is implicitly denied in an unmitigated loathing of "determined" matter, and the powers which rule are perpetually suspected of an alliance with the devil because they have consented to the creation of such a loathsome world. Heaven is at least at seven removes from the earth, and only begins where no more neighborly relations are possible. There are no real points of contact between divinity and the earth, which is not even touched by divine emanation. Reality is the sovereign domain of strangely unangelic angels, made up of Evil and hostility. The tedious task of the soul is, with much wisdom of initiation and often with cunning diplomacy, gradually to bypass the armies of angels and the strong points of Evil, and finally to slip into the remote kingdom of light.

The Castle of Kafka's novel is, as it were, the heavily fortified garrison of a company of Gnostic demons, successfully holding an advanced position against the maneuvers of an impatient soul. There is no conceivable idea of divinity which could justify those interpreters who see in the Castle the residence of "divine law and divine grace." Its officers are totally indifferent to good if they are not positively wicked. Neither in their decrees nor in their activities is there any trace of love, mercy, charity, or majesty. In their icy detachment they inspire certainly no awe, but fear and revulsion. Their servants are a plague to the village, "a wild, unmanageable lot,

---

[4] In the Cathedral chapter of *The Trial* the priest reproaches Joseph K. for seeking "too much help from others, especially from women" in his struggles to avoid his punishment.

ruled by their insatiable impulses . . . their scandalous
behavior knows no limits" (XV), an anticipation of the
blackguards who were to become the footmen of European dictators rather than the office boys of a divine
ministry. Compared to the petty and apparently calcu-
lated torture of this tyranny, the gods of Shakespeare's
indignation who "kill us for their sport" are at least ma-
jestic in their wantonness.

From the very beginning there is an air of indecency,
indeed of obscenity, about the inscrutable rule of the
Castle. A newcomer in the village, K. meets the teacher
in the company of children. K. asks him whether he
knows the Count and is surprised at the negative answer: " 'What, you don't know the Count?' 'Why should
I?' replies the teacher in a low tone, and adds aloud in
French: 'Please remember that there are innocent children present' " (I). And, indeed, what an abhorrent
rule it is! The souls of women seem to be allowed to
enter the next realm if they surrender their bodies, as
a sort of pass, to the officials. They are then married off
to some nincompoop in the village, with their drab existence rewarded only by occasional flashes of voluptu-
ously blissful memories of their sacrificial sins. Damnation is their lot if they refuse, as happens in the case
of Amalia, Barnabas's sister, who brought degradation
upon herself and her family by declining the invitation
of the official Sortini.

No, the Castle does not represent, as some early interpreters believed, divine guidance or even Heaven itself.
It is for K. something that is to be conquered, something
that bars his way into a purer realm. K.'s antagonism
to the Castle becomes clear from the very first pages of
the book. This is how he responds to the first telephone
conversation about his appointment which, in his presence, is conducted between the village and the authori-

ties: "K. pricked up his ears. So the Castle had recognized him as the Land Surveyor. That was unpropitious for him, on the one hand, for it meant that the Castle was well informed about him, had estimated all the probable chances and was taking up the challenge with a smile. On the other hand, however, it was quite propitious, for if his interpretation were right, they had underestimated his strength, and he would have more freedom of action than he had dared to hope" (I).

The correspondence between the spiritual structure of *The Castle* and the view of the world systematized into Gnostic and Manichaean dogma is indeed striking. There is, however, no reason to assume that Kafka had thoroughly studied those ancient heresies. In their radical dualism they are merely the model systems of a deep-rooted spiritual disposition, asserting itself over and over again in individuals and whole movements. Gnostic and Manichaean is, above all "the face that is filled with loathing and hate" at the sight of physical reality. Kafka refrains from any dealings with nature, such as are found, for instance, in his earliest story, "The Description of a Struggle." There is, apart from the mention of a starry sky, wind, and snow, not one description of nature in *The Castle*. Within the human sphere everything that is of the flesh is treated with a sense of nausea and disgust. All the habitations of men are lightless, airless and dirty. The nuptial embrace between K. and Frieda takes place amidst puddles of beer on the floor of a public bar, the room still filled with the stale smells of an evening's business, while mass prostitution is carried on in the stable of the inn.

But Kafka has also found subtler means of conveying his revolt against "matter." One evening K. is waiting in the dark courtyard of the inn for Klamm to emerge from his village room and enter his sled. The coachman, noticing K., encourages him to wait inside the sled and have a drink from one of the bottles kept in the side-pockets. K. opens the bottle and smells:

> Involuntarily he smiled, the perfume was so sweet, so caressing, like praise and good words from someone whom one loves very much yet one does not know clearly what they are for and has no desire to know, and is simply happy in the knowledge that it is one's friend who is saying them. "Can this be brandy?" K. asked himself doubtfully and took a taste out of curiosity. Yes, strangely enough it was brandy, and burned and warmed. How strangely it was transformed in drinking out of something which seemed hardly more than a sweet perfume into a drink fit for a coachman!
> (VIII)

Whether intentional or not, this profanation of the aroma of a spirit in the process of its being "realized" is a wonderfully subtle symbol of a Manichaean perspective on the world.

The Castle is, no doubt, the highest realm K. is capable of perceiving. This is what misled the critics, but not Kafka himself, into equating it with God. But it is certainly not quite irrelevant that in his personal confessions Kafka hardly ever utters the belief that the incessant striving of his spirit was directed toward God, or prompted by *amor Dei*. Almost all the time his soul is preoccupied with the power of Evil; a power so great that God had to retreat before it into purest transcendence, forever out of reach of life. Thus the idea of final authority, merely by assuming the shape of physical reality in *The Castle*, falls under the spell of Evil without the author's either willing it or being able to help it. It is the paradox of spiritual absolutism that the slight-

est touch of concreteness will poison the purest substance of the spirit and one ray of darkness will blot out
a world of light.

Although seemingly quantitative assessments of this
kind are always problematical, it is true that *The Castle*
is even more "Manichaean" than *The Trial*. Yet even
here it sometimes, if rarely, seems that the sinister
threat to the spirit, embodied in a senseless world, might
suddenly reveal itself as a disguised promise of happiness, a happiness and even goodness born of the non-
resistance to that world, indeed its resolute acceptance:
". . . you must take the side of the world." Although
the cursed rule of the Castle is the furthest point of
the world to which this wakeful mind can reach, there
dawns at its extreme boundaries a light, half-suspect-
ingly perceived, half-stubbornly ignored, that comes
from things outside the scope of Klamm's authority. K.
is possessed by only one thought: that he must come to
grips with Klamm; yet at the same time he knows that
his very obsession with this thought precludes him from
reaching what he mistakenly believes only Klamm can
give. He senses that if only he could renounce his consuming desire he would find what eludes him because
of his very striving for it. In Pepi, who for a short time
was promoted to the rank of barmaid in the local inn,
and thus enjoys the honor of serving beer to Klamm, K.
meets the caricatured personification of his own ambition. In giving her advice he shows a remarkable knowledge of his own malady:

> It is a job like any other, but for you it is Heaven,
> consequently you set about everything with exag-
> gerated eagerness . . . tremble for the job, feel
> you are constantly being persecuted, try by means
> of being excessively pleasant to win over every-

one who in your opinion might be a support to
you, but in this way bother them and repel them,
for what they want at the inn is peace and quiet
and not the barmaid's worries on top of their own.

And later:

When I compare myself with you . . . it is as if
we had both striven too intensely, too noisily, too
childishly, with too little experience, to get something that for instance with Frieda's calm and
Frieda's matter-of-factness can be got easily and
without much ado. We have tried to get it by crying, by scratching, by tugging—just as a child tugs
at the tablecloth, gaining nothing, but only bringing all the splendid things down on the floor and
putting them out of reach for ever. (XX)

But it is in K's adventure with the Castle official
Bürgel that this insight finds its most striking expression. K., summoned in the middle of the night to an
interview with the official Erlanger, has, in his weariness and exhaustion, forgotten the number of the door,
and enters another room—more in the sleepy hope of
finding an empty bed there than an official of the Castle.
There he encounters Bürgel. The ensuing dialogue, or
monologue rather, is one of Kafka's greatest feats in the
art of melting the solid flesh of a grotesque reality and
revealing behind it the anatomy of the miraculous.
Bürgel promises K. to settle once and for all his affairs
in the Castle. K. is not in the least impressed by this
offer. He waves it aside as the boast of a dilettante:

Without knowing anything of the circumstances
under which K.'s appointment had come about, the
difficulties that it encountered in the community
and at the Castle, of the complications that had
already occurred during K.'s sojourn here or had
been foreshadowed, without knowing anything of

all this, indeed without even showing, what should have been expected of a secretary, that he had at least an inkling of it all, he offered to settle the whole affair up there in no time at all with the aid of his little note-pad.

It is the unbelief of a labyrinthine mind in the very existence of simplicity. And while K. grows ever more weary, Bürgel delivers, in a rapturous crescendo, the message of the miracle: If a man takes a secretary of the Castle by surprise; if, in the middle of the night, the applicant, almost unconscious of what he does, slips, like a tiny grain through a perfect sieve, through the network of difficulties that is spread over all approaches to the center of authority, then the Castle, in the person of this one secretary, must yield to the intruder, indeed must almost force the utterly unexpected granting of his request upon the supplicant: "You think it cannot happen at all? You are right, it cannot happen at all. But some night—for who can vouch for everything?— it *does* happen." It is an event so rare that it seems to occur merely by virtue of rumor, and even if it does occur, one can, as it were, render it innocuous "by proving to it, which is very easy, that there is no room for it in this world" (XVIII). And Bürgel goes on with his rhapsody, describing the shattering delight with which a secretary responds to this situation. But when he ends, K. is sound asleep and, with the conditions of the miracle fulfilled before his eyes, as unaware of its possibility as he had been in his tortured wakeful pursuit of it.

Indeed, no comfort can be found *within* this world. Yet the power not only to experience but poetically to create this world must have its source *outside*. Only a mind keeping alive in at least one of its recesses the memory of a place where the soul is truly at home is able to contemplate with such creative vigor the struggles of a man lost in a hostile land; and only an immensity of goodness can be so helplessly overcome by the vision of the worst of all possible worlds. This is the reason why we are not merely terrified by the despair of this book but also moved by its sadness, the melancholy of spiritual failure carrying with it a hardly perceptible faith, the very faith of which all but inexhaustible resources are needed, as Kafka believed, for merely carrying on the business of every day.

In one of his most Manichaean sayings—in "Reflections on Sin, Suffering, Hope, and the True Way"— Kafka speaks of the power of a single crow to destroy the heavens; but, he adds, this "proves nothing against the heavens for the heavens signify simply: the impossibility of crows." And although these birds swarm ceaselessly around *The Castle*, its builder built it from the impulse to render them impossible. Is it, one wonders, yet another phantom hope in a deluded world that prompts in the book a child, a simple girl, and a wretched family to turn with a mysteriously messianic expectation to the Land Surveyor K.? And makes, in one version of Kafka's attempt to continue the unfinished manuscript, an old woman say of the homeless stranger: "This man shouldn't be let go to the dogs." Or is it perhaps the reflection of a faith, maintained even in the grip of damnation, a faith which Nietzsche once expressed: "Whosoever has built a new Heaven, has found the strength for it only in his own Hell" (XV, 393)?

SHORT BIBLIOGRAPHY

Stories and Collections of Stories
Published during Kafka's Lifetime

Betrachtung. Leipzig: Rowohlt, 1913.
Das Urteil. Eine Geschichte. Leipzig: Kurt Wolff, 1913.
Der Heizer. Ein Fragment. Leipzig: Kurt Wolff, 1913.
Die Verhandlung. Leipzig: Kurt Wolff, 1915; 2d ed., 1918.
In der Strafkolonie. Leipzig: Kurt Wolff, 1919.
Ein Hungerkünstler. Vier Geschichten. Berlin: Verlag Die
   Schmiede, 1924.

Works Published after Kafka's Death

Der Prozess. Berlin: Verlag Die Schmiede, 1925.
Das Schloss. Munich: Kurt Wolff, 1926.
Amerika. Munich: Kurt Wolff, 1927.
Beim Bau der Chinesischen Mauer. Ungedruckte Erzäh-
   lungen und Prosa aus dem Nachlass. Max Brod and Hans
   Joachim Schoeps, eds. Berlin: Gustav Kiepenheuer, 1931.
Vor dem Gerstz. Collected by Heinz Politzer from Kafka's
   writings. Berlin: Schocken, 1934. (Bücherei des Schocken
   Verlags, No. 19.)

Collected Works in German

Gesammelte Schriften. Max Brod, ed. (in cooperation with
  Heinz Politzer).
  Erzählungen und kleine Prosa. Berlin. Schocken, 1935.
  Amerika. Berlin: Schocken, 1935.
  Der Prozess. Berlin: Schocken, 1935.
  Das Schloss. Berlin. Schocken, 1935.
*Beschreibung eines Kampfes. Novellen, Skizzen, Aphorismen
  aus dem Nachlass.* Prague: Heinrich Mercy Sohn (acting
  as agent for Schocken), 1936.
Tagebücher und Briefe. Prague: Heinrich Mercy Sohn, 1937.
Tagebücher 1910–1923. New York: Schocken Books, 1951.
Briefe an Milena. Epilogue, Willy Haas, ed. New York:
  Schocken, 1952.
*Hochzeitsvorbereitungen auf dem Lande und andere Prosa
  aus dem Nachlass.* Frankfurt am Main: S. Fischer Lizenz-
  ausgabe, 1953.
Beschreibung eines Kampfes. Die zwei Fassungen. Epilogue,
  Max Brod, ed. Text-critical ed., Ludwig Dietz. Frankfurt
  am Main: Fischer, 1969.
Briefe 1902–1924. Max Brod, ed. Frankfurt am Main: S.
  Fischer Lizenzausgabe, 1958.
*Briefe an Felice und andere Korrespondenz aus der Verlo-
  bungszeit.* Erich Heller and Jürgen Born, eds. Introduc-
  tion, Erich Heller. Frankfurt am Main: S. Fischer Lizenzausgabe, 1967.

*Editions of Kafka's Works in English Published in New York
by Schocken and in England by Secker and Warburg*

The Great Wall of China, Stories and Reflections. Willa and
  Edwin Muir, trans. Exegetical Notes by Philip Rahv. 1946;
  new ed., 1970.
Amerika. Willa and Edwin Muir, trans. Preface, Klaus
  Mann; Afterword, Max Brod. Copyright 1946, by New
  Directions. Published by Schocken in 1962 in association
  with New Directions.
The Penal Colony. Stories and Short Pieces. Willa and Edwin
  Muir, trans. 1948.
Diaries, 1910–1913. Max Brod, ed. Joseph Kresh, trans. 1948.

Diaries, 1914–1923. Max Brod, ed. Martin Greenberg, with the cooperation of Hannah Arendt, trans. 1949.
Letters to Milena. Willy Haas, ed. Tania and James Stern, trans. 1953.
Dearest Father: Stories and Other Writings. Ernst Kaiser and Eithne Wilkins, trans. Notes, Max Brod, 1954. (In England: *Wedding Preparations in the Country and Other Posthumous Prose Writings.*)
Description of a Struggle. Tania and James Stern, trans. 1958.
Parables and Paradoxes/Parabeln und Paradoze. Bilingual ed. Nahum N. Glatzer, ed. 2d expanded ed., 1961.
Letter to His Father/Brief an den Vater. Bilingual ed. Ernst Kaiser and Eithne Wilkins, trans. 1966.
The Metamorphosis/Die Verwandlung. Willa and Edwin Muir, trans. 1968.
The Trial. Willa and Edwin Muir, trans. Rev. ed., with additional material translated by E. M. Butler. With excerpts from Kafka's *Diaries.* Drawings by Franz Kafka, 1968.
The Complete Stories. Nahum N. Glatzer, ed. 1971.
Letters to Felice. Erich Heller and Jürgen Born, eds. James Stern and Elisabeth Duckworth, trans. Introductory Essay, Erich Heller. New York, 1973.

Biographies, Memoirs, Bibliographies

Beicken, Peter U. *Franz Kafka: eine kritische Einführung in die Forschung.* Frankfurt am Main: Athenaion, 1974.
Benson, Ann. "Franz Kafka: An American Bibliography," *Bulletin of Bibliography*, XXII, No. 5 (1958).
Brod, Max. *Franz Kafka: Eine Biographie.* Frankfurt am Main: S. Fischer, 1962. (*Franz Kafka: A Biography.*) 2d, enlarged ed., including additional chapter, "New Aspects on Kafka." G. Humphreys Roberts and Richard Winston, trans. New York: Schocken, 1960.
Flores, Angel, and Swander, Homer, eds. *Franz Kafka Today.* Madison: University of Wisconsin Press, 1958.
Heller, Erich, and Beug, Joachim, eds. *Dichter über ihre Dichtunger: Franz Kafka.* Munich. Heimeran/S. Fischer, 1969.
Hemmerle, Rudolf. *Franz Kafka—eine Bibliographie.* Munich: Lerche, 1958.

Janouch, Gustav. *Gespräche mit Kafka*. Frankfurt am Main: 1968. (*Conversations with Kafka: Notes and Reminiscences.*) Introduction, Max Brod. Goronwy Rees, trans. New York: 1953.

————. *Franz Kafka und seine Welt: Eine Bibliographie*. Vienna: 1965.

Järv, Harry. *Die Kafka-Literatur: Eine Bibliographie*. Malmö und Lund: Bo Cavefors, 1961.

Jonas, Klaus W. "Franz Kafka: An American Bibliography," *Bulletin of Bibliography*, XX, No. 9 (1952), and XX, No. 10 (1953).

University of Wyoming, Kafka Seminar of 1972. "Franz Kafka Bibliography: 1960–1970." *Research Studies*, 40 (2 and 3), Pullman, Washington, 1972.

Wagenbach, Klaus. *Franz Kafka. Eine Biographie seiner Jugend (1883–1912)*. Bern: Francke, 1958.

————. *Franz Kafka in Selbstzeugnissen und Bilddokumenten*. Reinbeck bei Hamburg: Rowohlt, 1964.

Books in English on Kafka

Anders, Günther. *Franz Kafka*. A. Steer and A. K. Thorlby, trans. London: Hillary House Publications Ltd., 1960.

Eisner, Paul. *Franz Kafka and Prague*. New York: Arts, Inc., 1950.

Goodman, Paul. *Kafka's Prayer*. New York: Vanguard Press, Inc., 1947.

Gray, Ronald. *Kafka's Castle*. Cambridge: Cambridge University Press, 1956.

————. *Franz Kafka*. Cambridge: Cambridge University Press, 1973.

Greenberg, Martin. *The Terror of Art: Kafka and Modern Literature*. New York: Basic Books, 1968.

Neider, Charles. *The Frozen Sea: A Study of Franz Kafka*. New York: Oxford University Press, 1948.

Politzer, Heinz. *Franz Kafka, Parable and Paradox*. Ithaca: Cornell University Press, 1962, 1966.

Sokel, Walter H. *Franz Kafka*. New York: Columbia University Press, 1966.

Tauber, Herbert. *Franz Kafka: An Interpretation of His Works*. G. Humphreys Roberts and Roger Senhouse, trans. New Haven: Yale University Press, 1948.

Thorlby, Anthony. *Kafka: A Study*. London: Rowman and Littlefield, 1972.

Urzidil, Johannes. *There Goes Kafka*. Harold A. Basilius, trans. Detroit: Wayne State University Press, 1969.

INDEX